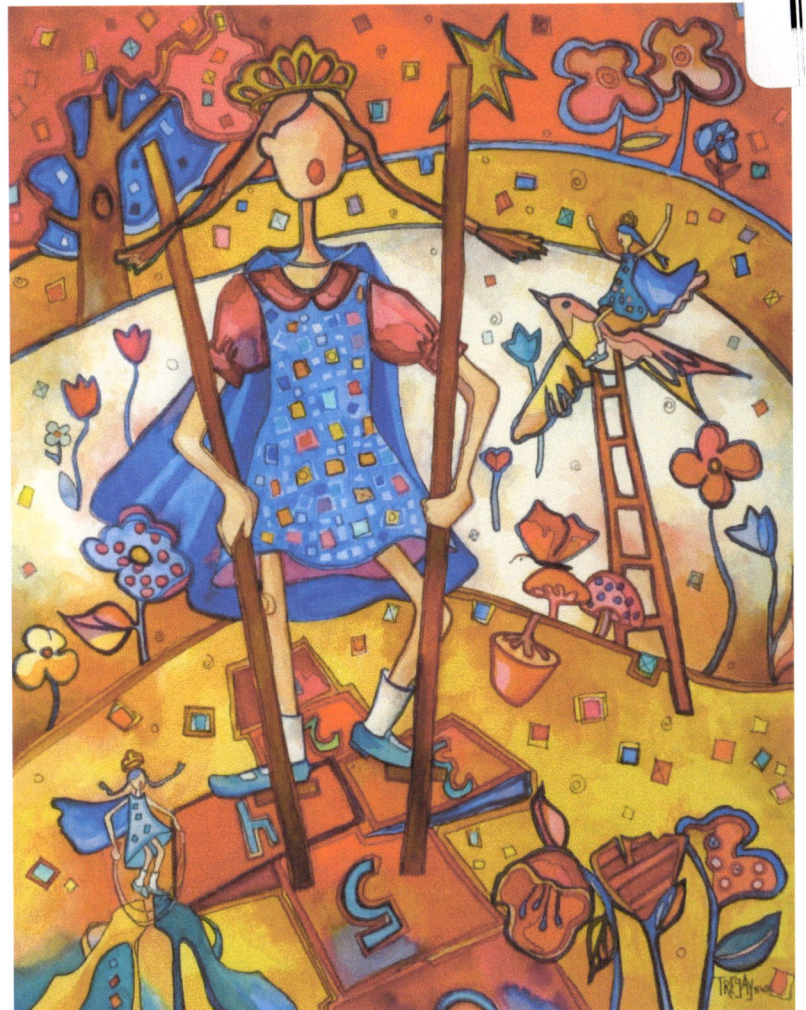

2000 Painting Titles
Create. Add Content. Polish Your Work.

Susan Webb Tregay AWS, NWS
George W. Tregay

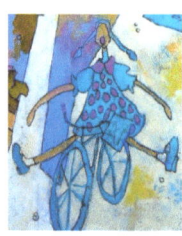

© 2018 Susan Webb Tregay and George Tregay

All rights reserved. This book may not be reproduced in any manner without written permission.

Susan Webb Tregay, AWS, NWS
57 Skyline Drive Ext.
Hendersonville, NC 28791
swtregay@aol.com

ISBN: 978-1985370074

All paintings are by Susan Webb Tregay AWS, NWS.

Cover "When Phones Were Heavy and Stayed Home" (detail), 24 X 24, acrylics on canvas; title page "Once Upon a Time There Were Free-Range Children," 30 x 22, watercolor.
For more information about the author, please visit SusanWebbTregay.com.

Design by Sarah Tregay
Author photo by Beth Beasley DeBona courtesy of the *Times-News*.

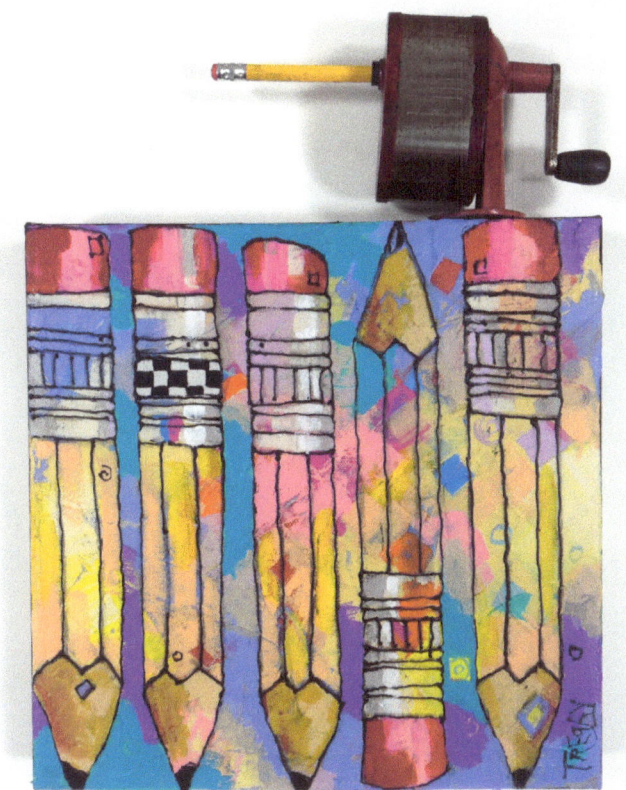

"These Are Not Pencils,"
10 x 10, acrylics on
canvas with pencil and
sharpener

Table of Contents

Playing Without Rules	1
Now or Never—Word Pairs	3
Tossed Salad—Fill in the Blanks and Mix and Match	7
True Fiction—The Grand List	11

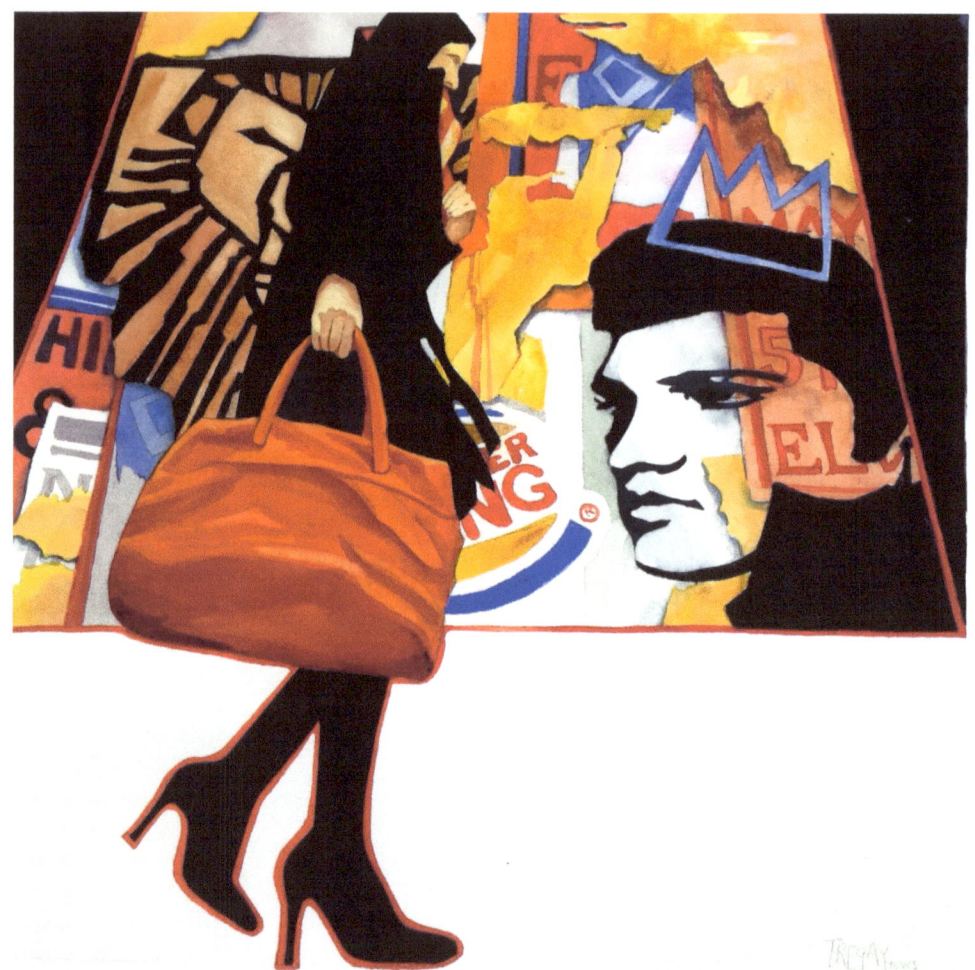

"The Kings and I," 25 x 22, watercolor

Playing Without Rules

Wonderful titles will help you connect with your inner thoughts and motives for creating a personal work of art. They can direct a painting at any step along the way as well as give it polish, surprise and finishing touches at the end.

Titles help clients connect with your paintings. Non-artists sometimes need word clues. They operate on the verbal side of their brain, the left side. You can give them a head start in appreciating your work by choosing an exciting title.

I use the list in this book for three jobs. Firstly, certain titles, say "America Woman," jump start my imagination! I never have to ask myself "what will I paint today?" I can pull out this list and, bingo, there are dozens of ideas sitting there for the taking.

Often I use this book at the mid-point of a painting. Choosing a title then helps direct me to how I want to express myself, what mood I'm aiming for, and how I personally feel about the topic. This is what is meant by content. Content is everything in art!

Lastly, the perfect title can nail down your painting in your own mind, while giving a viewer, soon to be a client, an understanding of the work that they may not have come up with on their own.

My husband and I created and collected these titles over the past twenty years from our experiences and reading, as well as from music and book titles. Titles are not copyrightable, so feel free to use them to create, move a painting along and to polish a finished piece. Or use this list to jog your memory and create a new title of your own.

We have left plenty of white space for you to write in your own title ideas. Write in the crazy ones as well and the gems. Make *2000 Painting Titles* your personal studio necessity.

Silent Attraction—Using This Book

When I start a painting, I sit down with my sketchbook and references and pull out this book and read through it—for the thousandth time. Next, I jot down five or six possible titles in my sketchbook. Some might be ordinary, some weird and some funny. The stranger the better. One might be perfect, but that is unusual. It's the funny ones that finally generate the ideal title. Then I start to paint.

I always consider if it is possible to subtly use the title, or words from the title, in the actual work. What images does a prospective title bring to mind? Can these images become part of the painting and add intellectual depth to the piece?

Finally, I choose a title, or adapt one from the initial five or six.

When I begin the next painting that series, I can go back to this page in my sketchbook and already have possible titles listed to inspire, use or adapt to the next painting in the series.

You will find that working with *2000 Painting Titles* will generate new titles and ideas. Add new possible titles directly into this book. When you reading and a great title pops into your mind, add it as well. Make this book your own.

The List

We will begin this book with the simple idea of word pairs and then stretch your brain to the Mix and Match section. Then your creative self will be ready for the Grand List. Jump in. It's now or never.

Now or Never—Word Pairs

Sometimes the content in paintings is helped along by the use of words in the actual piece. Putting your thoughts and feelings into paintings can be difficult, and words offer a simple solution.

These word pairs may give you some ideas. They can be used as abstract elements in backgrounds, subtle and barely readable. Or they can add surprise to storefronts and street signs in cityscape paintings. How can you use words to enhance the meaning behind your paintings?

As/Was
Back/Then
Begin/End
Belief/Doubt
Come Together/Fall Apart
Coming/Going
Crisis/Opportunity
Either/Or
First Place
Five/Dime
Future/Past
Give/Take
He Knew/She Knew
Here/Hence/There
Here/Now
Here/There
Hide/Seek
High/Low

Hillbilly Drive
If/Only
In/Out
Inhale/Exhale
Inside/Out
Late/Early
Late/Never
Look/See
Looking/Seeing
Lost/Found
Me/You
Message/Reply
Milky Way
Music/Noise
Music/Silence
My/Way
New Life/No Instructions
Nice Place

No Beginning/No End
No/Yes
Not So/Fast
Now!/Now?
Now/Never
Now/Then
Nowhere/Anywhere
Open/Shut
Our Place
Out/About
Ozzie/Harriet
Past/Future
Past/Present
Present/Tense
Question/Answer
Ready/Not
Remember/Forget
Remote/Recent
Safe/Sorry
Scene/Unseen
See/Be Seen
Seen/Unseen
Sense/Nonsense
Shout/Whisper
Shouts/Whispers

Spelling/Misspelling
Splish/Splash
Start/Finish
Stop/Here
Talk Whisper
Terms/Conditions
Their/Way
Then/Again
Then/Now
There/Now
This Way/ That Way
Together/Apart
Truth/Fiction
Until/Now
Until/Then
Up/Down
Was/Will
Watching/Waiting
Way/Ahead
Way/Back
Yes/Know
Yes/We Have Grits
You/Me
Way Out

> **WARNING:** Our eyes identify and latch onto letters and words fast and hard. You probably don't want words to be either be your center of interest or a distraction from your carefully composed painting. Words will always dominate and create a heavy weight in balancing a design. Use them judiciously and obscure them so that they are barely readable.

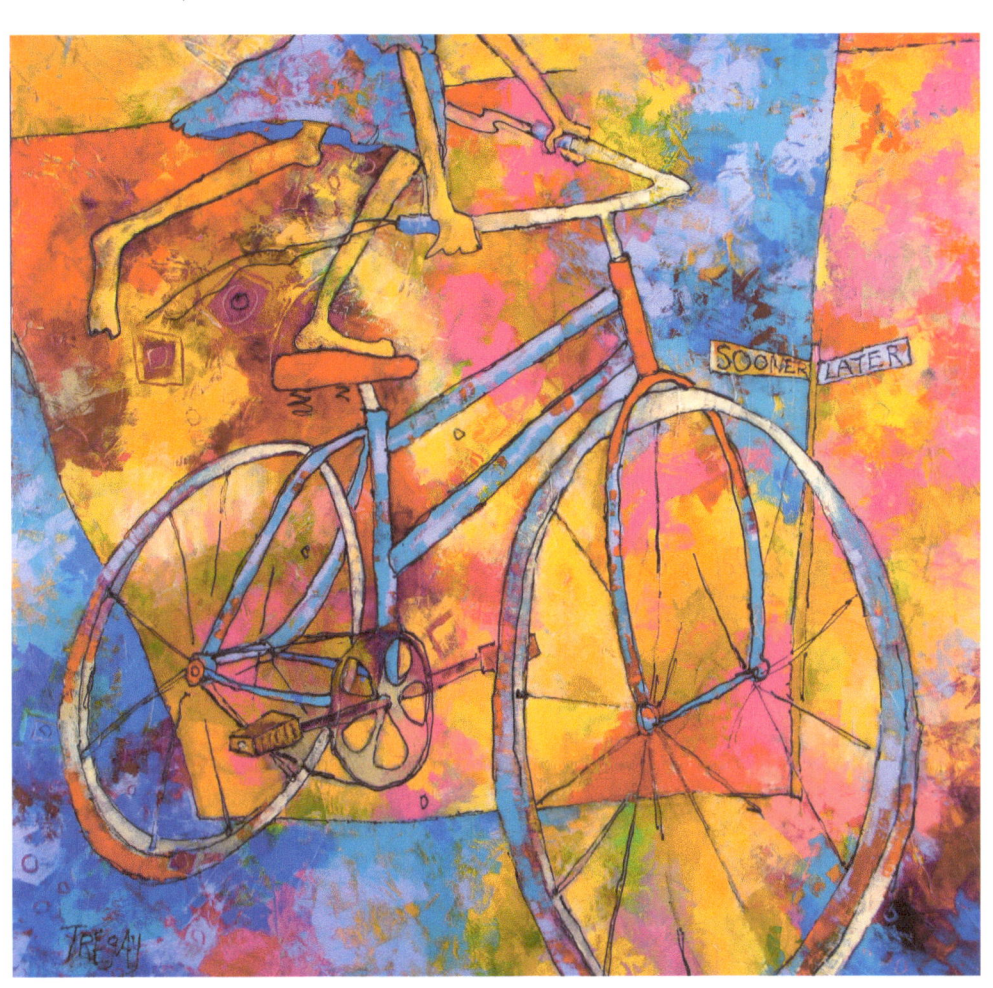

"Sooner or Later," 24 x 24, acrylics on canvas

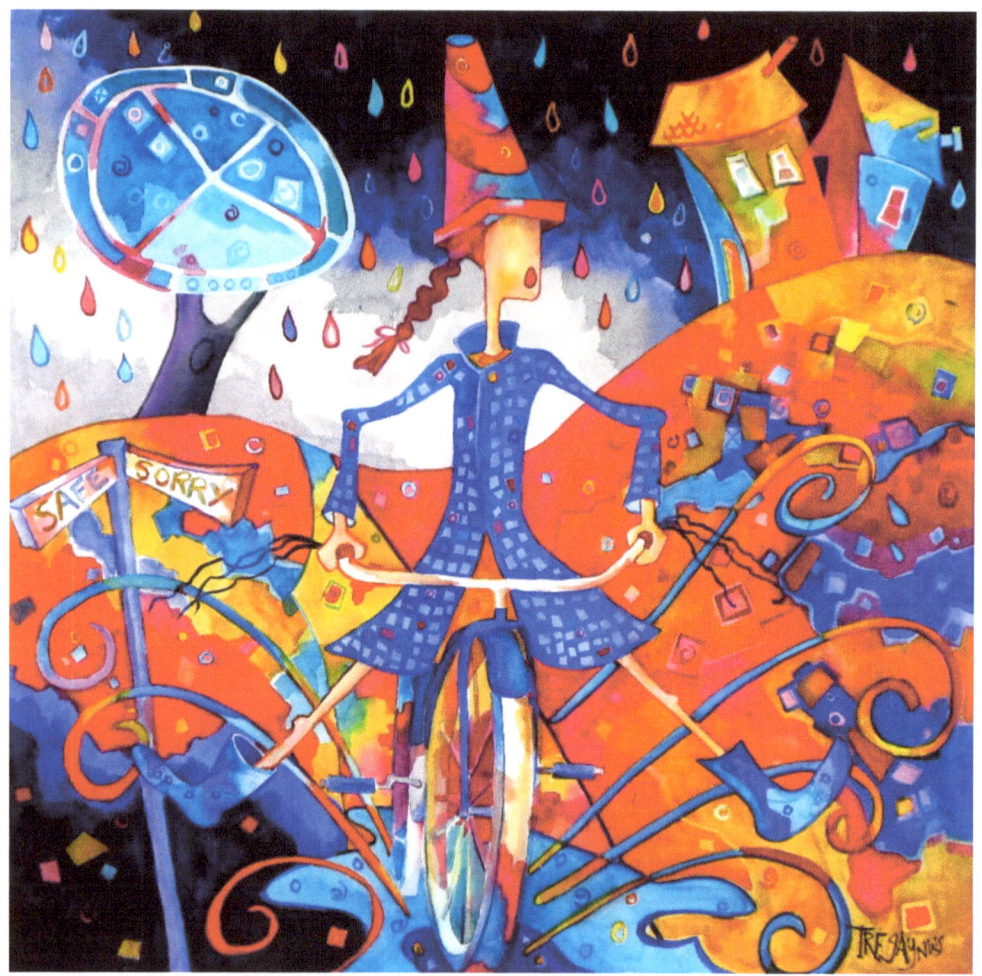
"Before the Age of Anxiety," 22 x 22, watercolor

Tossed Salad — Fill In the Blanks and Mix and Match

The purpose of this book is to inspire you to paint (or finish a painting) with the intention of expressing something about yourself—content.

I started this title list after reading that Jackson Pollack named his paintings by randomly choosing words from two lists. Random words obviously worked for Pollack's abstract work, but you don't want to waste an opportunity to reveal your intentions to your viewer.

This section will inspire you to generate titles that can do so much more: "Touchy Recollections, "When in Drag," "Before the Age of Anxiety." Let your mind wander. What will you come up with?

A Sound Like…	…And Clean Up Your Room
Abundant…	…and Jive
Dialogue with…	…and Bach and Blues
Edge of…	…Birthday
Future Classic…	…Bistro
I Loved You…	…But Then Again
Impeccable…	….Recollections
Introducing…	…Quakes
Inventing the…	…of the Real
Laughing…	…Recognition
Leaving… (Brookline, etc.)	…Resume
Letter to…	…Seldom Blink
Lights, Camera, …	…Time
Monsieur…	…to Boot
My Name is…	…Café
Odyssey and…	…Congregating (houses, flowers, etc.)

Quiet....

Raising...

Refuge from ...

Rescuing...

Say Nice Things About... (Detroit, Jane, etc.)

Self-Portrait with...

Substitute...

Suspending...

Stream of...

Still...(a name)

The Allure of...

The Book if...

The Last...

The Secret Life of ...

The Truth About...

The World According to ...

The Age of ...

The Girls from ...

The Neighborhood...

Touchy...

Trivial...

Untitled #...

Uppity...

Undertones of...

Unresolved...

Waking for ...

Western...

When in ...

When in Rome...

The Rules of...

They Don't Write Songs about...

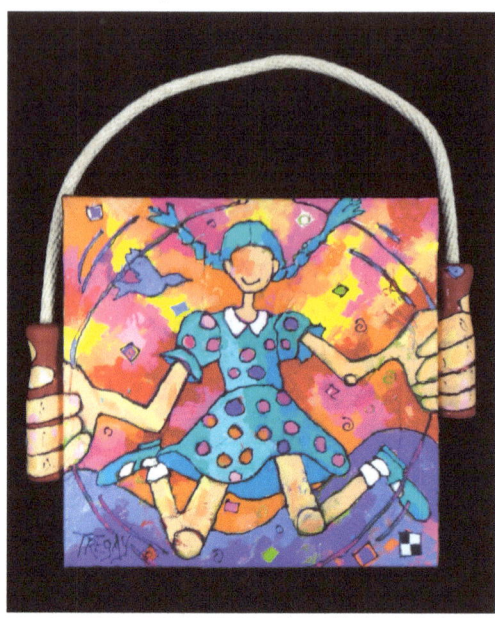

"Pepper," 10 x 10, acrylics on canvas with jump rope

...Discussion

...in Disgust

...Encounter

...Envy

...for Beginners

...from the Get Go

...in the Age of Anxiety

...in a Blender

...in Drag

...in Disgust

...in December

...Invite Comparison (brothers, roses, etc.)

Sounds Like ... To Me

If / When ... was the Rage

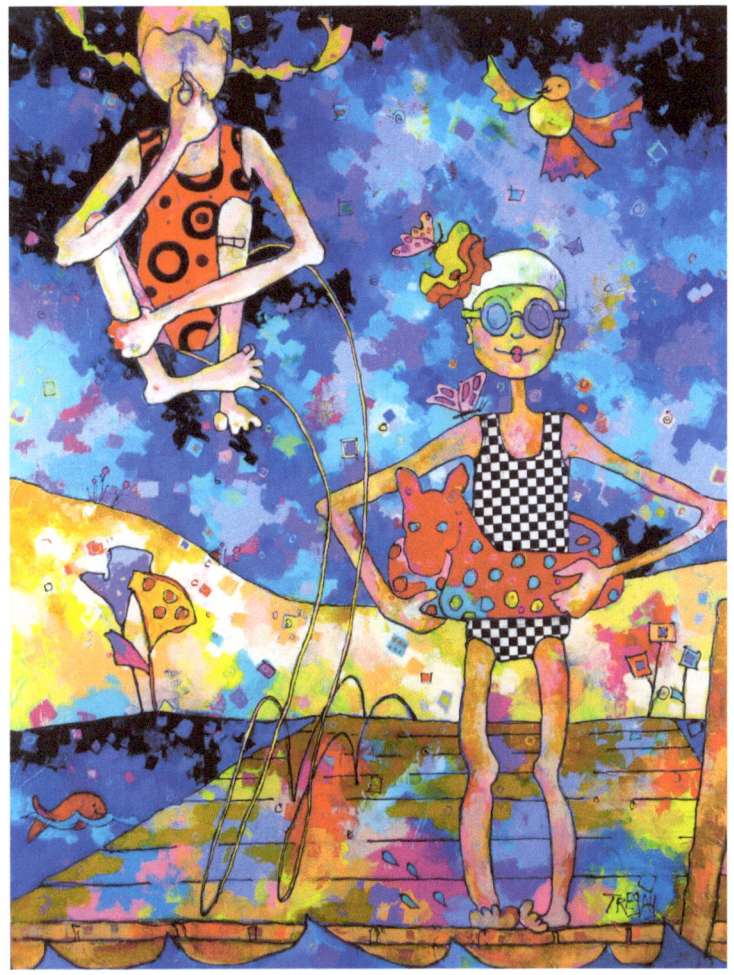
"The Optimist and the Pessimist," 40 x 30, acrylic and fabric on canvas

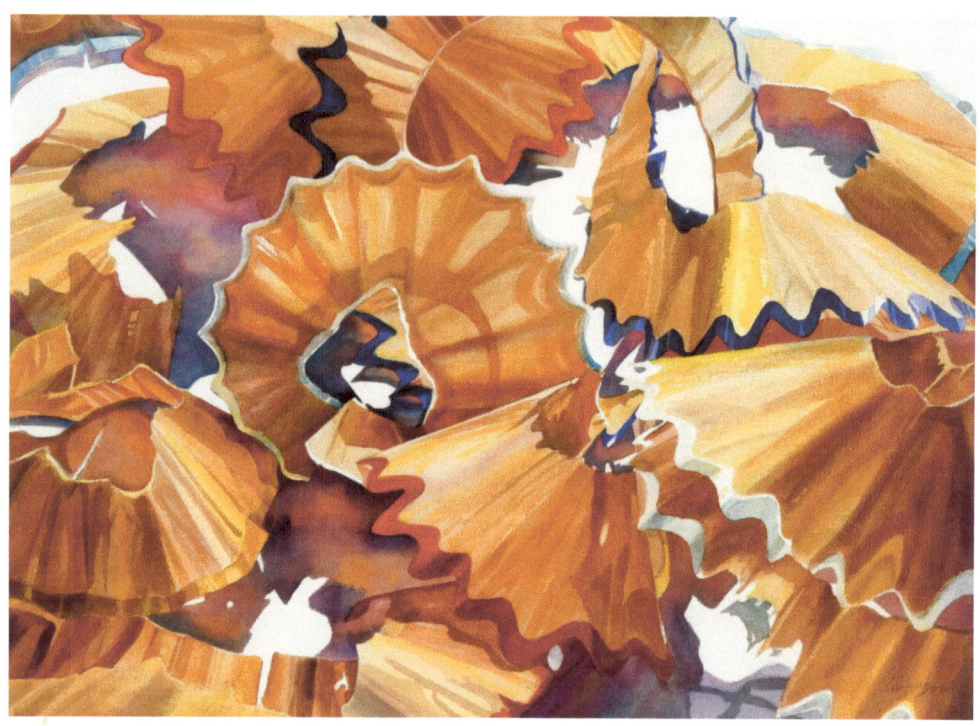
"What We Leave Behind," 22 x 30, watercolor

True Fiction—The Grand List

This list is a jumping off point to help you generate new and better titles. You may use it to inject humor into your life and the lives of your clients. A great title will give your paintings depth and create new understanding in what otherwise might be ordinary subject matter.

Read the list over and over as you develop each new painting. Add your own ideas directly into this book. Make this book indispensable.

1964, The Last Year of Innocence
2 or 3 Things I know for Sure
20 Rules on How to Paint the Nude
9/10 of the Law
90 Degrees With 100% Humidity
911
A Bedroom in Venice
A Believer in Good Enough
A Changed Man
A Door is Not a Window
A Downtown Radical
A Different Time Zone
A faint, cold fear/ thrills through my veins.
(William Shakespeare)
A Fine Blend (of journalism and acupuncture)
A Girl I Knew

A Goal is a Dream with a Deadline
(Eva Hesse)
A Great Place to Die
a la Mode
A Legend in his own Lunchtime
A Lie Uncovered
A Lie Undetected
A Life in Vermilion
A Lifetime In His Eyes
A Memoir
A Mirror With a Memory
A Moment of Madness
A Piece of My Heart
A Place I've Never Been
A Place of Our Own
A Rigged System
A Single Essence
A Sound Like Thunder

A Time Now Gone
A Touch of Love
A Tune Without Words
A Victim of My Own History
A Window is Not a Door
A Woman's Place is in the Wrong
(James Thurber)
A Year Without Fall
About Love
Absent
Absent Friends
Abstract Diary
Abundant Irony
Accelerate
Accidental Environmentalist
Accidental Woman
Accidentally on Purpose
According to What?
A-Changin' Times

Act Your Age
Actual Reality
Actual Size
Adult Education
Adult Supervision
Adult Themes
After
Affordable Perfume
After the CE
Afterglow
Afterimage

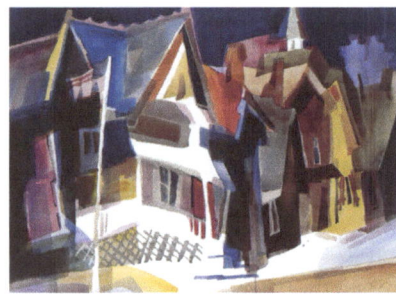

"I Grew Up Surrounded by Republicans,"
22 x 30, watercolor

Afterthought
Age of Anxiety
Age of Aquarius *(A Memory of Great Music and Love)*
Agree to Disagree
A House With No Mirrors
Ain't We Got Fun?
All Hat and No Cattle
All Men Are Mortal
All Rise
All She Ever Wanted

All the Better to See *(Hear, Taste)* You with, My Dear
All the Right Answers
All Together Now
All We Had Was Rock and Roll
Altar of Abstraction
Altitude
Always Under Foot
American Camouflage
American Dream
American Essays
American Girl
American Heros
American in Paris
American Memory
American Perspective
American Style
American Woman
An American Diary
An Echoey Lack of Emotion
An Enabling Fiction
Analyze This
Anecdote in a Jar
Animal Magnetism
Annual Memory
Another Country
Another Life
Another Way
Answer Yes or Know
Any Boy Can Grow Up to be President
(Any Date)

Any One Can Become an Icon (As Long as They Have the Right Outfit)
Anything for Billy
Aperture Setting F8
Approaching
Approximation of the Truth
Are We there Yet?
Arrested Development
Arrivederci
Art in the Garden
Art is Long, Time is Fleeting *(Henry Wadsworth Longfellow)*
Artful
Artist
Artistic License
As It Should Be
As Seen on TV
As We Were Saying
Ask About my Tattoos
Assisted Evolution
Astonish Me From a Different Gene Pool
Attitude
Audible Silence
August 14, 1942
Available Light
Babes
Baby Boomers
Back and Forth
Back in the Game
Back Then
Back to Basics

Back to Square One
Back to the Wall
Back When We Were Grown-ups
Bad Publicity
Balls
Banal Memories
Based on a True Story
Basic Black
Batty Housewife
Be Nice
Because
Becoming Who We Are
Been There
Been There, Seen That
Before Bucket Seats
Before Color TV
Before Minivans
Before Plastic
Before Polyester
Before the Age of Anxiety
Below the Radar
Better Late Than Never
Betty Crocker
Between Art and Life
Between Light and Dark
Between Parentheses
Between Spaces
Between the Lines
Beyond
Beyond Reason

Beyond Recall
Beyond the Box
Beyond the Rectangle
B-film
Birthday Party
Big News
Bizarre
Black and White
Blind Date
Blossoms Falling
Blue Angel
Blue Grass
Blue Light
Blue Light Special
Blue Melody
Blue Moon Café
Blues
Body of Knowledge
Body of Work
Body Surfing
Born in a Cage Too Small *(Indira Ghandi)*
Borrowed Light
Borrowed Time
Boundaries: Respected and Crossed
Bourgeois Guilt
Bowling Alone
Braided Branches
Braided Lives
Braving the Elements
Breaking Camp

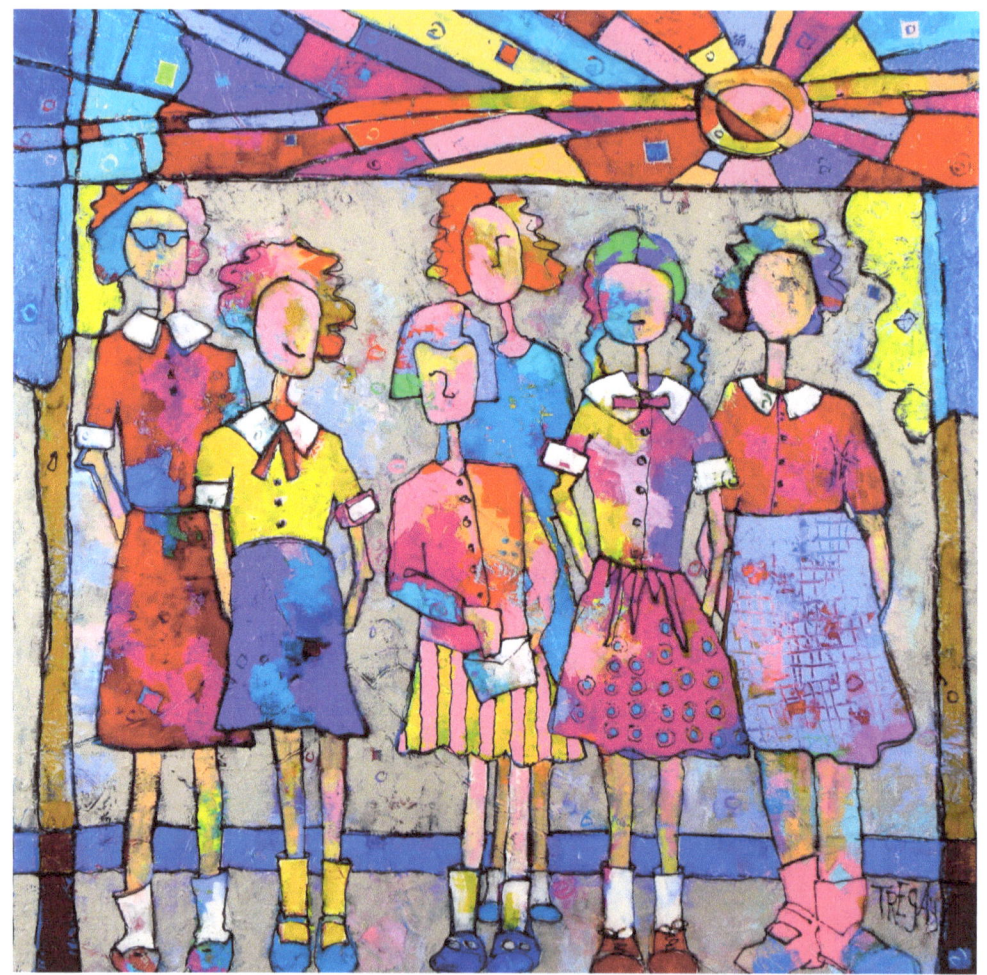
"The Baby Boomers," 24 x 24, acrylics on canvas

Breathing Room
Breathing Secondhand Pot
Breathless
Bringing Back the Draft
Broken House(s)
Brush strokes
Buildings that Twist and Turn and Ache
Bullfrog Blues
Burst of Laughter
Business as Unusual
But is it Art?
But Seriously
Butterfly Wings
Butterscotch
Buzz Words
By a Thread
By Nightfall
By Reason of Gender
By the Slice
By the Way
Cabin Fever
Call and Response
Call Waiting
Calling Out
Camouflage
Camouflaged Life
Can We Resolve This?
Can You Hear Me?
Candlelight

Canyon Suite
Canyon Sunset
Carnival
Carnival Act
Carnival of Lilies
Carnival Performer
Carnival Tricks
Carousel of...
Carless Memory
Cast of Characters
Cat's Cradle
Catch and Release of Time
Caught Inside
Central Time
Certified Copy
Cha, Cha, Cha
Change of Heart
Change of Plans
Change of Seasons
Changing Faces
Changing Paradigms
Changing Seasons
Changing Weather
Chapter 2
Characters *(as in letters)*
Charade
Charleston Fusion
Chasing Shadows
Chasing the Foreseeable Future
Chat Room
Checkered Past

Checklist
Checks and Balances
Cheery Normalcy
Cheesy Lyrics
Chewing the Fat
Chill Out
Chinese Character for "Crisis" Also Means "Opportunity"

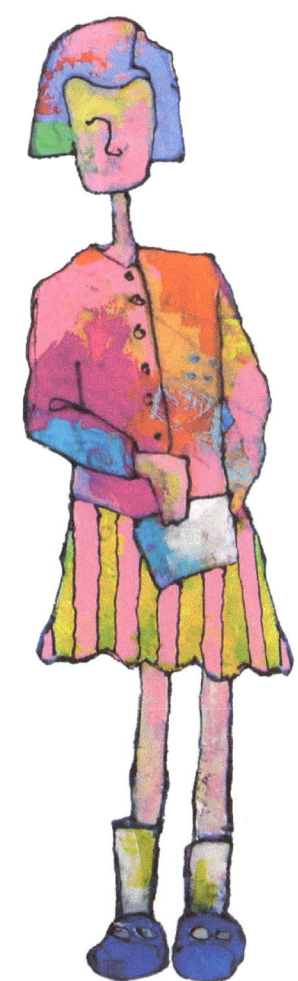

Chronic Symphonies
Circles on the Lawn
Circles in the Water
Circular Logic
Circular Reasoning
Circumstantial Landscape
Circumstances
Clear Conscience
Cliff Hanger
Climate Controlled
Closed Circle
Closing of the Door
Closing Time
Club Sandwich
Cold Shoulder
Cold Reality
Collected Metaphors
Color Me Impressed
Color Theology
Color.com
Colors on Line
Com Post Modern
Comic Release
Coming Home
Coming of Age
Coming Over for Passover
Common–Temporary
Complements
Completely Beside Ourselves (myself)
Compliments
Complements
Compulsive Activity
Con Temporary
Conceptual Cyberspace
Conceptual Fragments
Conceptual Karaoke
Congenital Preppies
Contagious Color
Contemplative Silences
Contents Under Pressure
Conversation
Conversations
Convolution
Cornflower Blue
Corner Office
Coronary Candidates
Correspondences
Cost of Living
Costume Party
Costumes
Counterfeit Necessities
Counting Success in Small Change
Coy Koi
Crayola Charleston
Crayola Garden
Crayola Sunset

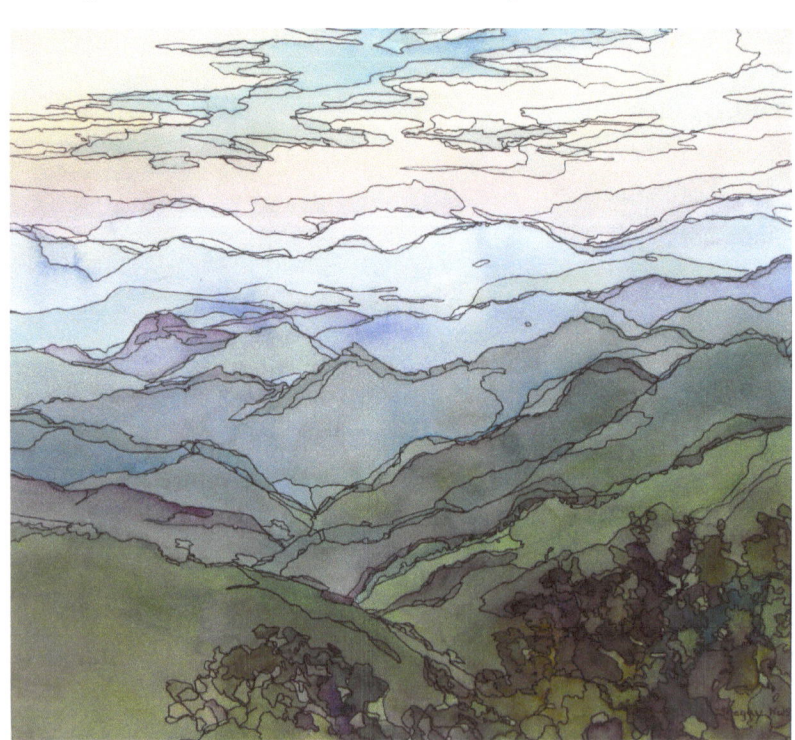

"Lost Satellite Reception," 15 x 15, watercolor and ink

Crazy Quilt
Credo Quia Absurdum
  (I believe because it's absurd.)
Crime Scene
Crimson Skies
Critical Condition
Critical Faculties
Crossing the Line
Cruise Control
Cruising
Cruising Altitude
Cultural Coding
Cultural Deterioration
Curious Artifacts
Cut it Out
Cute Clothes are Chilly
Cyber Orange
Daddy's Girl
Dancing by Myself
Dancing Garden
Dancing in the Street
Dancing to the TV
Dare Me
Dare to be Brave
Daughters of Grant Wood
Daylight Savings Time
Daytime TV
De FINE Art
Death by Gardening
Debatable
Decision Tree
Decisions

Decisive Distinctions
Defining Moment
Denial and Deception
Departure Lounge
Designing Woman
Destination
Destiny
Detours
Devil in the Blue Dress
Dialogue
Dialogue in the Past Tense
Dialogue with Charleston
Dialogue with Myself
Dialogue with the Past
Dichotomy
Dictionary of Imaginary Places
Die Trying
Difficult Job, but Someone Has to Do It
Digression
Dilemma
Dinner at the Homesick Diner
Diplomatic
Disappearing Act
Disappearing into a Book
Discussing Unmentionable Things
Dislodged Memories
Dismantled Memories
Disney Day
Distant Thunder
Distilled Spirits

Disturbance in the Field
Disturbing the Peace
Delicates
DNA
Do Not Abandon Me
Doctored Drawing
Dodging Memories
Dodging Realism
Dodging Reality
Does She...or Doesn't She?
Doing Charleston
Domestic Landscape
Domestic Vacation
Don't Bogart that Joint, my Friend
Don't Chase the Foreseeable Future
Don't Shoot the Messenger
Don't Tell
Don't Tell Dad
Don't Want to Talk About That
Double Exposure
Double Vision
Doublespeak
Drag is a State of Mind
Drawn Out Conversation
Dreams Are Faster than Dreamers
Dress Casual
Dress Code
Dress in Orange
Drop Dead Gorgeous

Dry Spell
Dubious Honor
Due Date
Durable Goods
Early visit
Earthly Possessions
East
Eastern Standard Time
Eat Your Heart Out Milton Bradley
Eclipse
Edge of Light
Educating Women
Eggplant Pizza
Eight Leaves of Grass
Elbow Room
Elegant Economy
Elegant Silence
Eleven Minutes
Elvis in the Morning
Empty Promises
Emptying the Fridge
Encounter
Endless Cycle
Enough Said
Envy
Epilogue
Episiotomies
Episode 3
Equal Affections
Equal Conviction
Equidistant

Escape
Essential Ingredients
Eternally Oblivious
Eternally Obvious
Etiquette
Evangelicals Seldom Blink
Eve was Framed
Evening Star Silver Moon
Every Movement Needs an Enemy
Everybody's Somebody's Baby
Everyone
Everything and More
Everything is so Easy for Pauline
Evidence of Our Times
Evidence of Other Times
Evidence of Things Unseen
Evil is Much More Banal than We Imagined
Except Where Prohibited
Excursion
Excuse Me
Exes
Exhaled Frustration
Exhibit A
Explorations
Express Lane
Extravaganza
Eye Contact
Eyeglasses *(as a metaphor)*
Eye to I

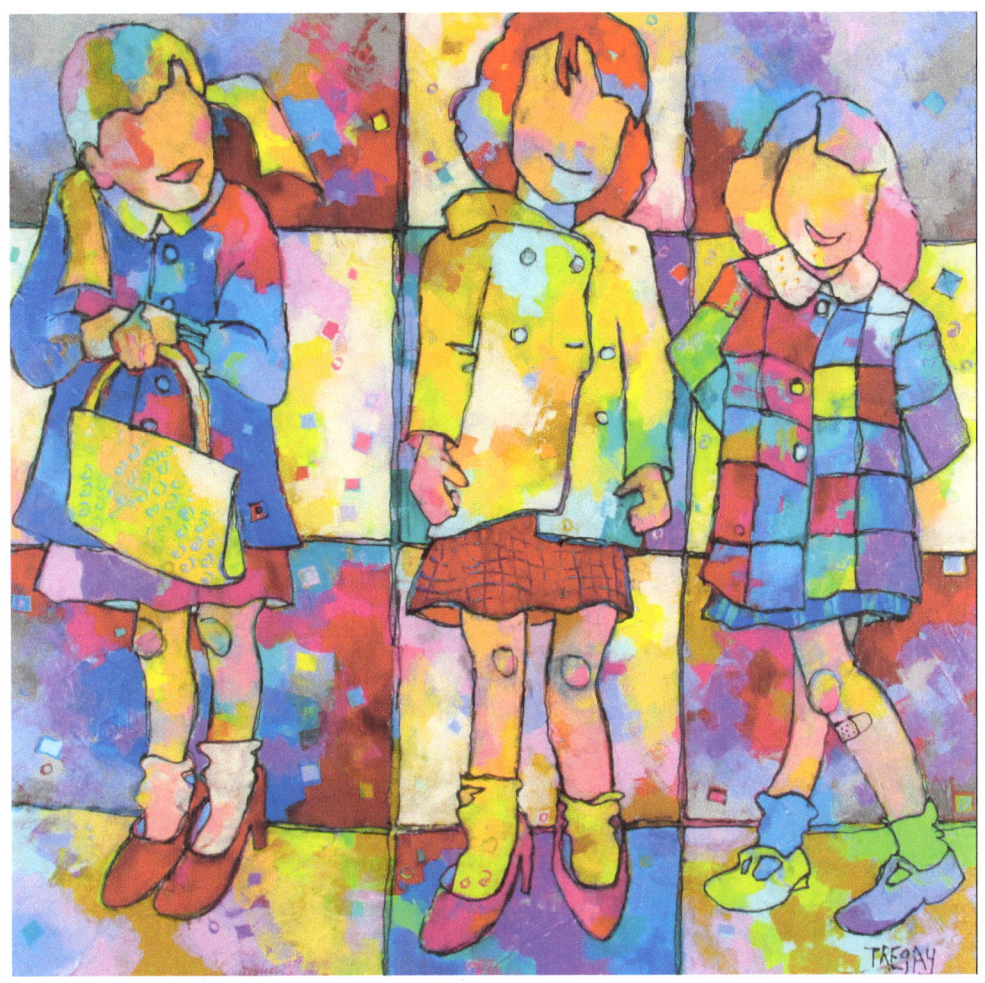
"Life Before Blue Jeans," 24 X 24, acrylics on canvas

Eyes on the Prize
Eyesight
Face to Face
Face Value
Facial Recognition
Fact of the Matter
Factual Enough
Fake News
Fake Reality
Fall Keeps on Happening
Falling Exceptions
Falling Expectations
Falling Feels Like Flying, for a Little While
False Start
Familiar Voices
Family Linen
Families and Survivors
Family Dancing
Family Reunion
Family Room
Family Surveillance
Family Tree
Fanatic Faction
Fatal Arrogance
Fate Keeps on Happening
Fearing the Bomb, Again
Feeling Around for my Shoes
Female Chauvinist Sow
Female Fetishes
Femme and Chicky
　(Ani Difranco)
Festival
Fiction
Fields of Gold
Figure of Speech
Figures of Speech
Fill in the Blank
Filling the Silence
First Impression

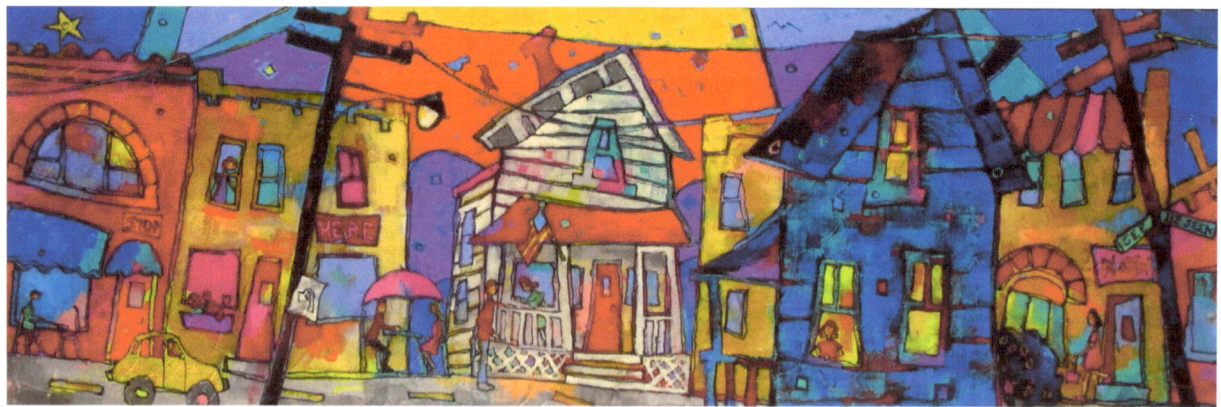

"Saturday Night," 12 x 36, acrylics on canvas

First One Out
Fits and Misfits
Flatscreen
Floating to the Surface
Fog
Floral Derangement
Flow
Focal Point
Following the Leader
Footnotes
Footnotes *(12 x 12 paintings)*
Foreseeable Future
Forest Essence
Forest Shelter
Forthcoming
Found Wanting
Fragile
Frame Up
Frankly Figurative
Frankly Iris
Free Love
Free Lunch
Freedom of Dissent
Frequent Flyer
Frequent Flyer Memories
Fresh Paint
Friends in High Places
Fuzzy Allegory
Flying Colors
Garden Evenings
Garden Fusion
Garden Party

Garden Quilt
Gate to the Sea
Gather
Gatherers of Stories
Generally Speaking
Gesture
Getting to the Point
Girl Meets Boy
Girl Scout Handbook
Glamour
Go Along to Get Along
Go Figure *(figurative painting)*
Going Back
Going Down Fast
Going Public
Good Advice: Fake Reality
Goodbye to Apple Pie
Goody Two Shoes
Gossip, the National Language
Gravity
Great American Whitewash
Green Circle
Greenery Without Irony
Greetings
Grit
Guess Who's Coming to Donner?
Guest Room
Guilt without Sex
Guilty is a Way of Life
Guilty, Liberal Democrat
Guises and Disguises

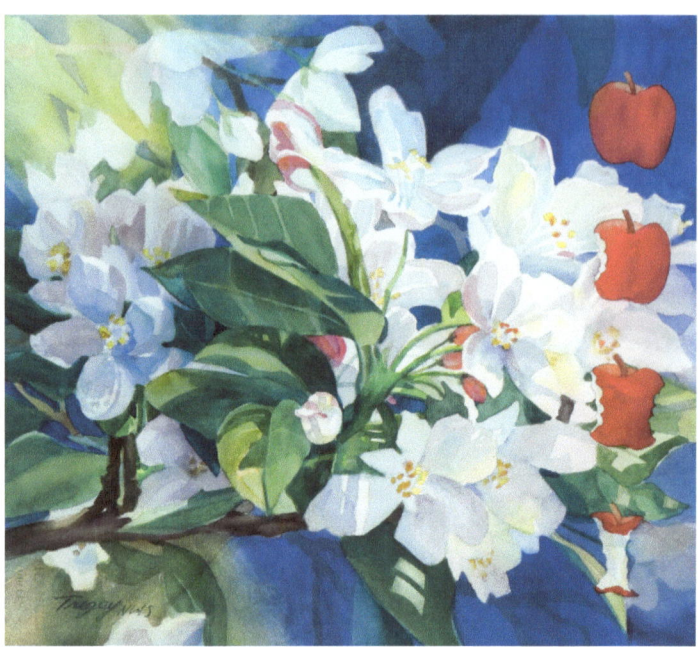

The Core of It, 22 x 24, watercolor

Half in Jest
Hallucinatory Realism
Happy Hour
Hard Edges
Hard Laughter
Hard to Swallow
Hardware
Harmony
Hats *(as a metaphor)*
Haunted
Haunted by Homer
Haunted Imagination
He Lost the Plot
He Said
He Wears High-Rise Pants
Head Lights and Tail Lights
Hear the Wind Blow
Heard it through the Grapevine
Heartquakes
Heat Wave
Heathen Liberal Traits
Held Back the Night
Help Wanted: Female
Hemingway's Girl
Here and Now
Here and There
Here, There and Everywhere
Herstory
Hi Fructose
Hidden Agenda
High Maintenance
Highkasies-Lokasies *(and other childhood rhymes)*
Hind Sight
Hindsight
Hippies Use Side Door
History is No Theme Park
Holding Back the Dawn
Home and Garden
Hoops
Hopelessly Morning
Hopelessly Post-Modern
Household Saints
Hot Blooded Girl
Hot Rock
Hot Stuff
Hot Ticket
Hotel America
Houseplants
House Rules
How Did You Get This Number?
How Do I Look?
How Does It Feel to be a Problem?
How Does Your Garden Grow?
How I Met Your Mother
How it Was
How the World Spins
How to Raise an Adult
How Was It?
Hubristic Folly

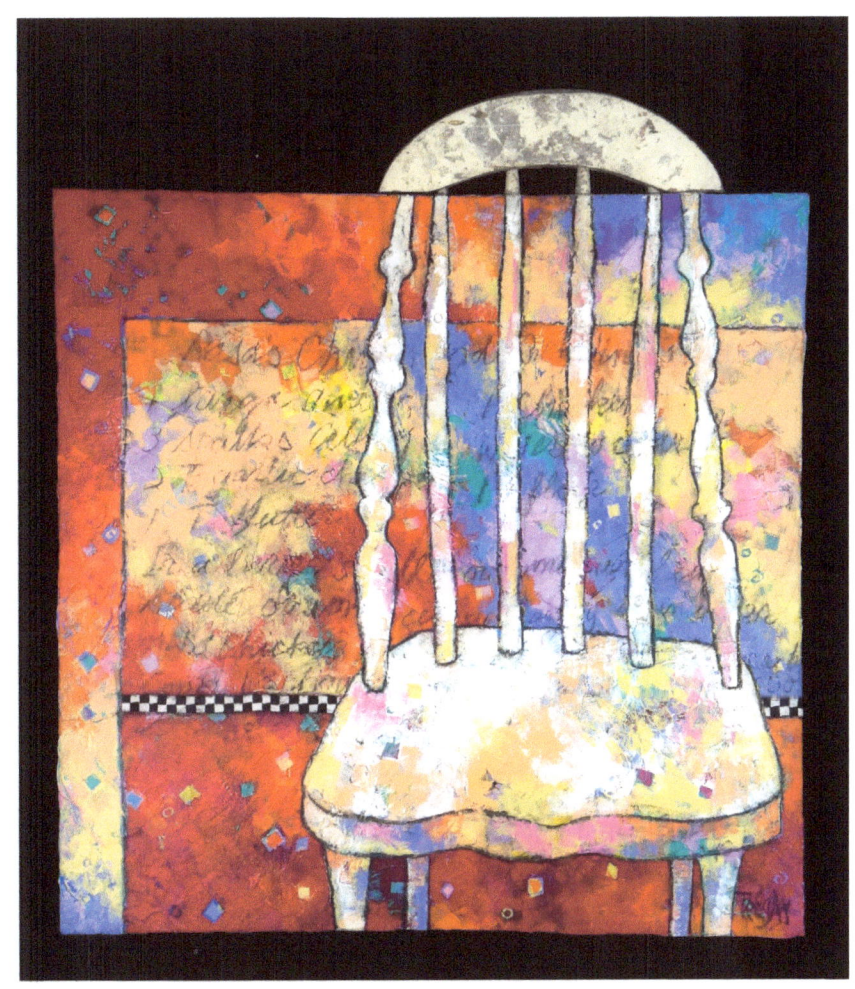

"Chicken and Dumplings," 24 x 24, acrylics on canvas with chair part

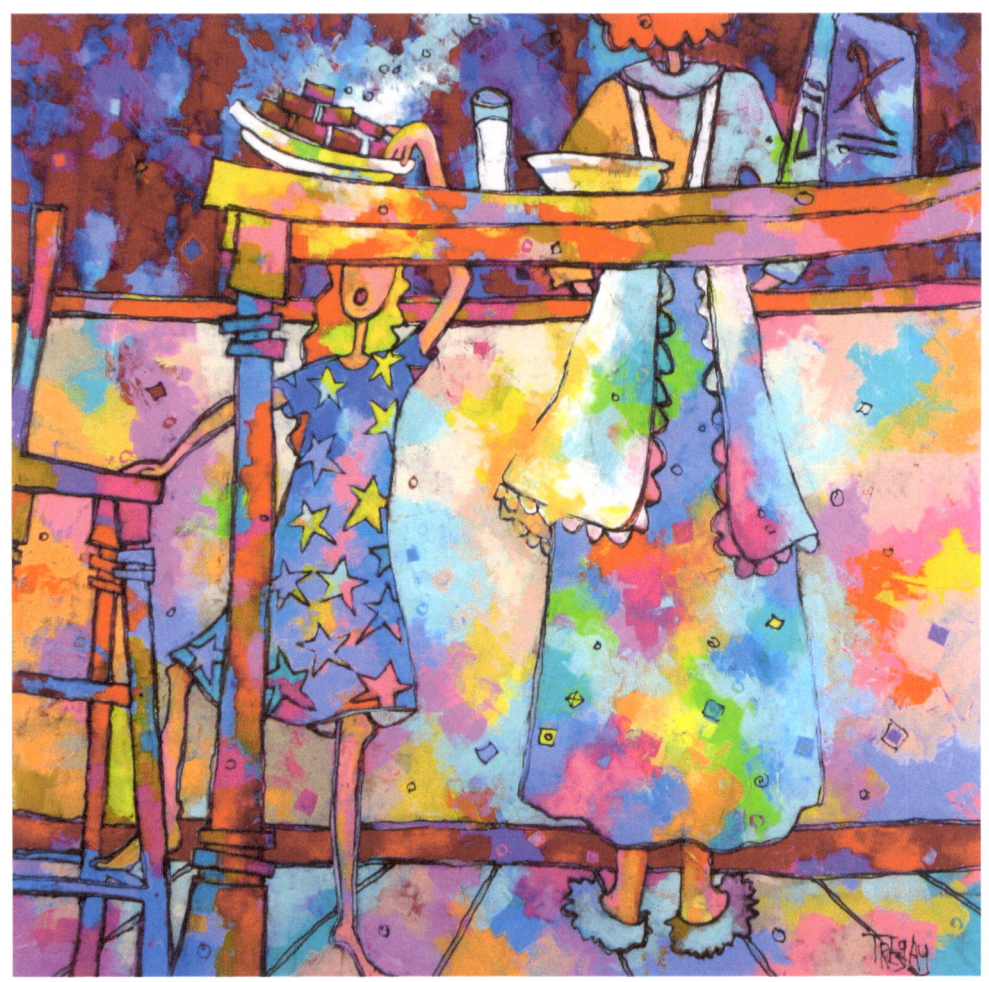

"Brownies for Breakfast," 24 X 24, acrylics on canvas

Hula
Hula Hoops
Human Nature
Hunters and Gathers
Hysteria
I am My Own Wife
I am No Shadow, I am a Wife *(Sylvia Plath)*
I am Watching You
I Don't Get It
I Gave Myself a Good Talkin' To
I Grew Up Surrounded by Republicans
(Im)possibility
(Im)possible
I Never Stopped Loving You
I Pulled Up My Bra Straps
I Remember my First Time
I Think It's the Heat
I Thought So
I Waited
I Want More than Biological Opportunity
I Was the Wrong Sex
I Was Told There'd be Cake
I Wish I May, I Wish I Might
I'll Be Seeing You
I'm Just Saying
Icon of the Past
Icons of the Moment
Icy
ID

If I Loved you, I Would Tell You
If You Want to Live Like a Republican, Vote Democratic
If Morning Ever Comes
If You're on a Budget, I Have Something Uglier
Impetuous
Impressionable
Improbabilities
Impulses
In and Out of Love
In Between the Lines
In Between the Sheets
In Her Own Skin
In Her Own Time
In My Anecdotage
In No Time
In Our Country, Guilty is a Way of Life
In Pursuit of Happiness
Insight
In Sight
In Sights
In Sites
In the House
In the Mood
In-Between Time
Incessant Criticism
Included in the Game
Incognito
Indigo Waters
Indivisible

Inevitable
Innuendo
Inside Job
Inside Out
Inside Looking Out
Inspiration Point
Integration
Interconnected
Interested Party
Interiors
Interrupting the Conversations I was Having in my Head
Interview
Intrigue and Confusion
Intuition
Inventing the... (Joneses)
Iris Awakening
Ironic Ambivalence
Ironic Awareness
Irrational Perspective
Is Anyone Taking Notice?
Is that So?
It Seemed Funny at the Time
It Seemed Like a Good Idea at the Time
It Was So French
It Was the Drink Talking
It Would Take an Invasion from Alpha Centauri to Bring Back the Draft
It's a Thin Line
It's About Me
It's About Time

It's Only Rock and Roll
It's the Law
Jack Kennedy didn't Sound Funny to Me
Jazz for the Carriage Trade
Jazz Fusion
Jet Lag
Jitterbug
Juice
Jumping Through Hoops
Junk Mail
Just Another Day
Just Desserts
Just like in the Movies
Just the Other Day
Just Thinking
Juxtapositions
Keep On Keeping On
Keep your Eyes on the Prize
Keeping House
Keeping Promises
Keeping Track of the Joneses
Keeping Up Appearances
Kick the Can
Kitsch
Kmart Realism
Know Me
L'Amour
Lackadaisical Attitude
Ladder to the Sky
Ladies with Options
Language

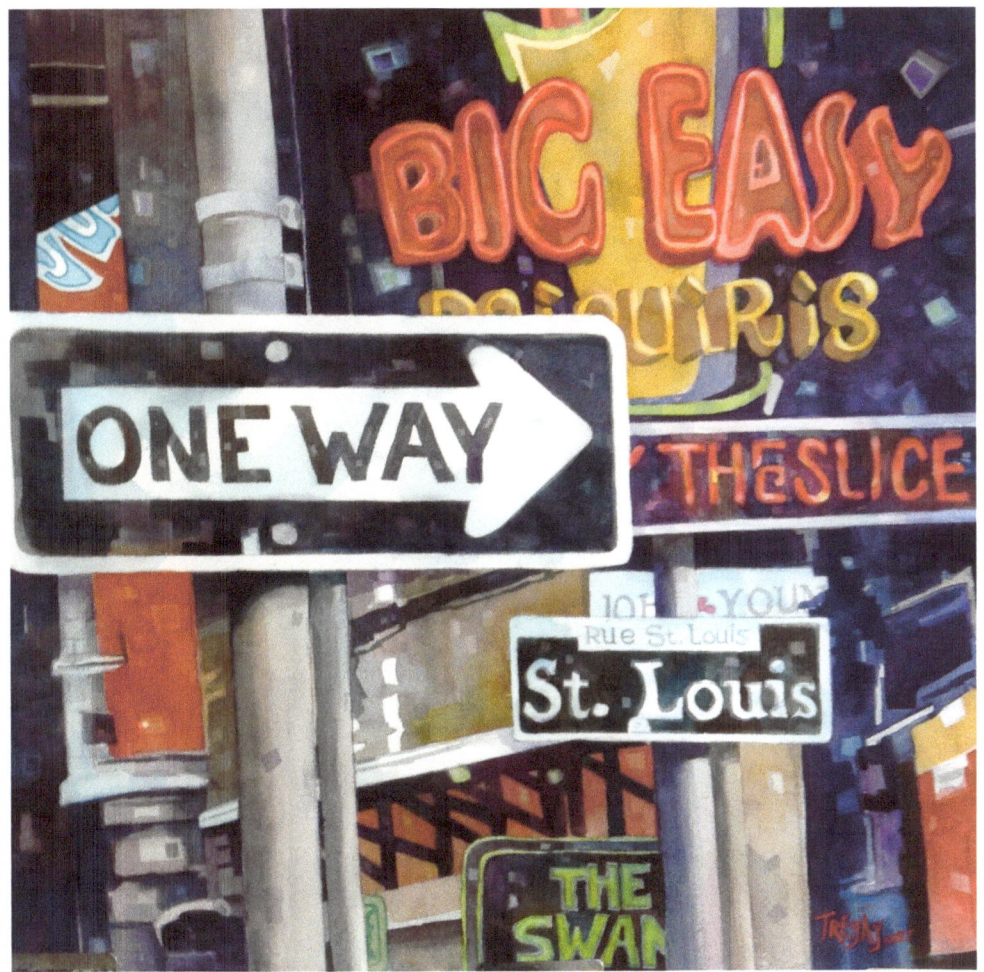
"The Big Easy," 22 x 22, watercolor

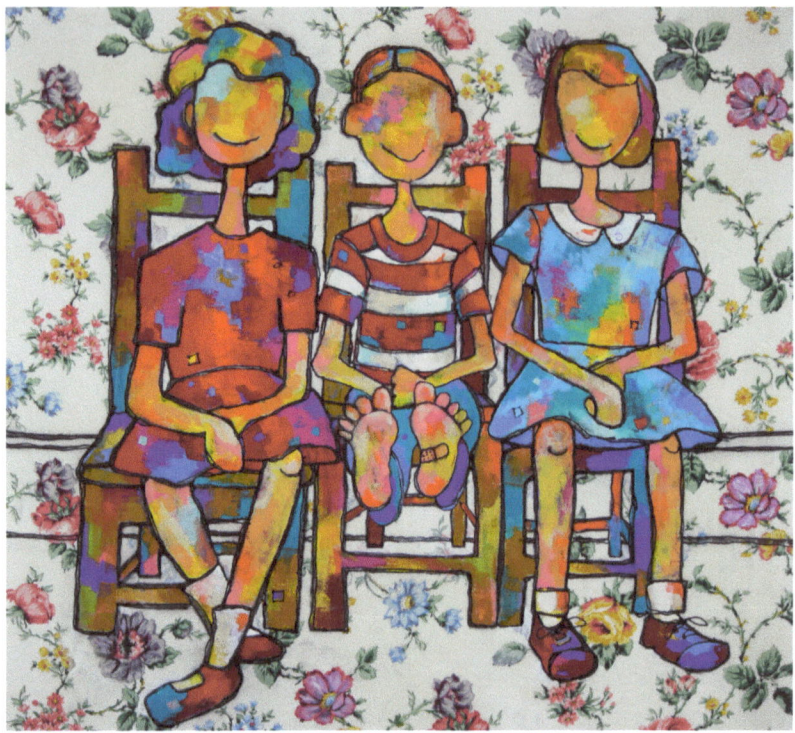
"Beside Ourselves," 24 x 24, acrylics on vintage fabric

Las Vegas is Our Versailles
Last Call
Last Season
Last Days Before the Internet
Late Bloomers
Late to Work
Laughing
Lawn Circles
Lazy Susan
Learned That the Hard Way
Leave a Message
Leaving on the Night Train
Leaving Time
Leap of Imagination
Left of Center
Left at the Light
Let It Be Morning
Letter in November
Liberal Arts
Liberal Studies
Lies of Silence
Lies we Tell Ourselves
Life After Winter
Life and Lies
Life Before Pizza
Life Before/After Blue Jeans
Life in Vermilion
Life is a Bitch, and it Starts in Third Grade
Life is a Contact Sport
Life on the D-list
Life Patterns
Life Support
Light Now
Lighthearted
Like
Like, Y'a Know, Whatever
Lily Culture
Lime and Orange.com
Liminal (Subliminal)
Limitations
Limited Visibility
Lip Reading
Listen Carefully As Our Options Have Changed
Listening to Billie
Literal Latte
Literary Devices
Little White Lies
Lives and Aspirations
Living a Still Life
Living in the Open
Living on Borrowed Time
Living Relics
Local Anesthetic
Local Artists
Locked into Boxes
Logic and Reason

Logic and Reason Banished
Lone Cone (flower)
Long Division
Long Nailed Women
Long Time Coming
Look at Ourselves
Look at Yourself, Look at Yourself
Looking Back, Walking Forward
Looking for Me
Looking for Signs
Looking for the Foreseeable Future
Looking Seeing
Looks are Deceiving
Loose Change
Lost
Lost Satellite Reception
Loud Silence
Loudly Silent
Love at First Books
Love and Other four Letter Words
Loving Care
Luck
Lucky
Lucky Break
Lucky Weekend
Lying in Bed
Lyrics
Magic, Mythology and Irrationality

Maintenance
Make Abbie Hoffman Quake in his Sandals
Making It a Home
Make it Home
Making Love with my Eyes Shut
Making me Famous
Making you Famous
Male Pattern Baldness
Manet Can't Buy You Love
Mansplaining
Mallspeak
Man-made Landscapes
Marching to the Beat of a Different Orchestra
Market-tested Sentiment
Married to My Conscience
Marry Well
Masked Memories
Master Disaster
Matthew Brady Ransomed
Maximalism
May You Live in Interesting Times
  (Chinese curse)
Maybe
Me and You
Meditation
Me and You and Everyone Else I've ever Known
Meanwhile and Far Away
Measurable Success

Medium Challenged
   (as a watercolorist)
Meeting Halfway
Mega Bytes
Melody
Memories About Memories
Men in Her Life
Menagerie
Metaphor-Free (Content Free)
Middle Ages
Mid-life
Milky Fog
Milton Bradley Ransomed
Mind your own Business
Minding Business
Minimum of Two
Minor Characters
Mirage
Mirror, Mirror on the Wall
Mirrors
Mischievous
Missing Chapters
Modified People (tattoos)
Monday's People
Money and How It Gets
   That Way
    (Henry Miller)
Monochrome
Monopolizing the Conversation
Monotone
Money Doesn't Grow on Trees
Moods

Moral Photographs
More Passion
More than You Know
Morning Dialogue
Morning Hours
Morning Light
Morning Realities
Mother Lode
Mother May I?
Mountain Time
Movie-going
Moving Pictures
Moving Water
Much Too Late
Multi-tasking
Music and Lyrics
Music and Silence
Mute Button
My Agenda
My American Life
My Backyard
My Girlfriend's Boyfriend
My Boyfriend's Girlfriend
My Dog Has Fleas
My Education
My Guilty Conscience
My Heart Still Beats in ¾ Time
My Life as a Sitcom
My Mother? I'll Tell You About
   My Mother
My Mother's Body

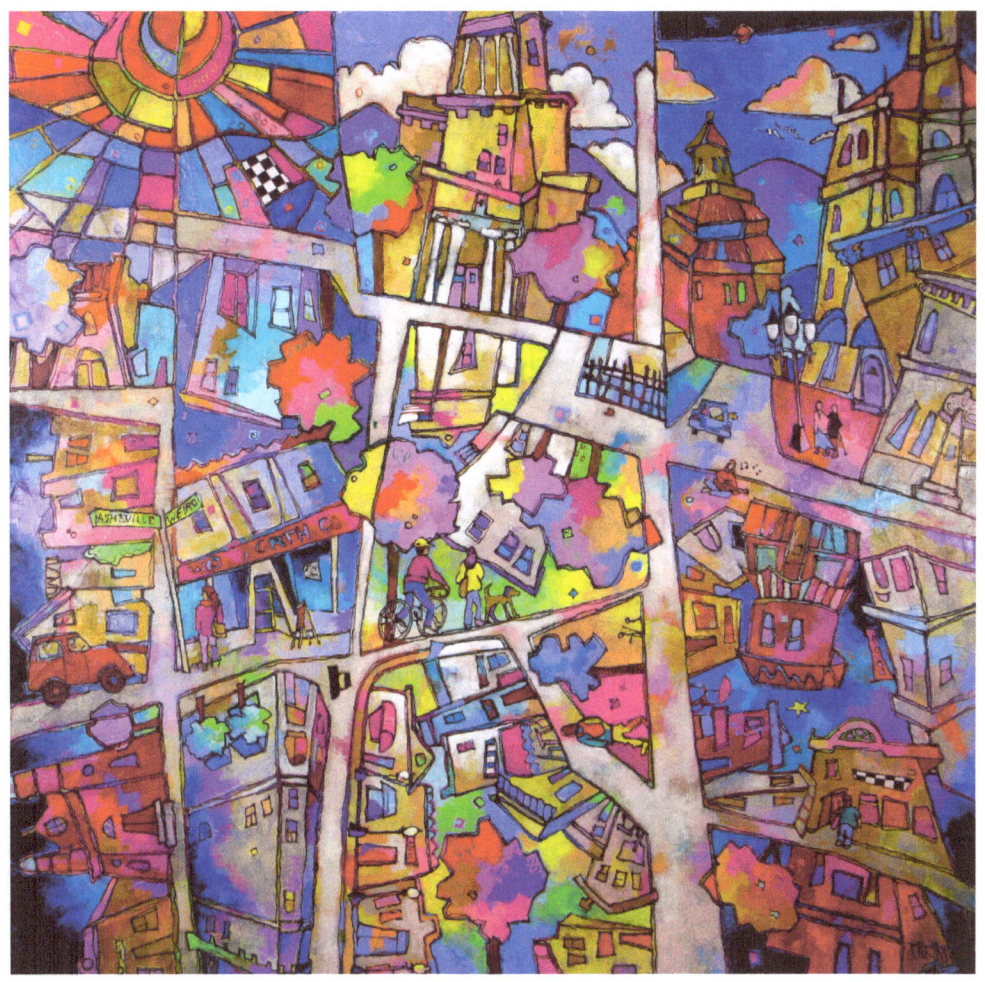
"Asheville, Life Outside the Lines," 36 x 36, acrylics on canvas

My Public Image
My sister Knows All
My Thighs
Nancy Drew
Narrative Fragments
Nashville
Natural Look
Navigate
Necessity's Mother
Neither a Subject Nor an Object
Netflix
Neither Here nor There
Neurotic Realism
Never Change
Never Charge
Never Go Back
Never Managing to Leave
Next of Kin
Next-door
Night Before Last
Night Frost
No Bonnie and Too Many Clydes
No Dirty Dancing Allowed
No End in Sight
No More Questions
No Parking
No Problem
No Regrets
No Right Turn
No Shortcuts

No Time
Nobody's Fool
Nocturne
Nonchalance
Nonchalant
Nonfiction
Nontrivial Pursuit
Noon
Normal is Not Good
North
Nostalgia Isn't What it Used to Be
Not Quite True
Not the End of the World
Not the Worst Painting I've Ever Done
Nothing Holds Back the Night
Nothing in Common

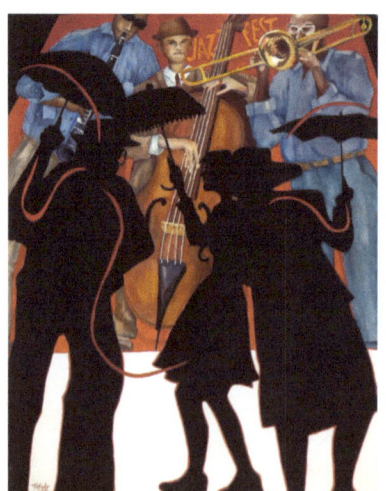
"Jazz Fest, Nawlins," 22 x 29 watercolor

Nothing Ironic Ever Happens to Me
Nothing Personal
Nothing to Get Hung About
Novel
November Light
Now This Won't Hurt a Bit
Nuances
Oblivion
Obsessive Realism
Obstruction
Off the Wall
Oh for Crying Out Loud
Old News
On Borrowed Time
On the Brink of Something
On the Edge of Time
On the Map
On the Road
On Their Own
Once a Week Won't Kill You
On the Road
Once Around the Block
One Day
One Hour
One Lump or Two
One More Day
One More Month
One of the Crowd
One of the Guys
One Summer Motionless

One Thing Leads to Another
Only Natural
Only the Rich Kids Dressed Poor
Only Tolerated
Oozes Attitude
Op-Ed
Open
Open House
Opening Soon
Open to the Public
Open to Suggestion
Operating Instructions
Optic Nerve
Optimistic Projections
Oral History
Orange.com
Ordinary Life
Ordinary Lives
Ordinary... (heroes)
Organic...
Other People's Children
Our Days
Our Lady of Perpetual Responsibility
Our National Subconscious
Out in the Open
Out of Character
Out of Context
Out of Order
Out of Print
Out of the Frame

Out of the Picture
Outside In
Outside Looking In
Outside the Lines
Outward Appearances
Over-aged Harlot
Overheard
Overlooked
Overtones
Pacific Standard Time
Paint by Number
Painting by Numbers
Painting in a Foreign Language
Painted Ladies
Paint by Numbers
Pale Males
Pale People
Panty Raids
Paper View
Paris Photo
Partially True
Passing Judgment
Passion for Action
Passive Aggressor
Passive-Aggressive
Past Caring
Past Tense
Patron Saint of Liars
Paul's Letter to the Buffalonians
Paying Attention
Peeking at the Foreseeable

Future	Picture of You
Pensive Speculation	Piece by Piece
Pentimento	Pink Menagerie
Peony Envy	Places I Have Been
People of Colors	Places I Have Never Been
People Who Wear Polyester (Are Clearly a Force to be Reckoned with) (*Stephen King*)	Plan B
	Plain Truth
	Planet B
Perfect Match	Play Acting
Perfect Lives	Play by Play
Perfect Pitch	Play music like you've never heard it before.
Perishable	
Perpetual Care	Play to the End
Perpetual Motion	Play Without Rules
Perpetuating Myths	Played Out
Perpetuating the 50s	Playing Dumb
Perpetuating the 50's Mythology	Plays Well With Others
	Pocket Fodder
Persistence of the Past	Poetic License
Persistent Image	Point of Departure
Personal Baggage	Point of View
Personal Drama	Political Landscapes
Personal Histories	Politics as Usual
Personal Mythology	Pop In
Personal Perception	Possible Palpitations
Personal Perspective	Post-Disney Perspective
Personal Velocity	Post-Everything
Perverted Geometry	Post-Modern Zeitgeist
Perverted Perspective	Post-Partum
Petal Pushers	Postponed
Pfft	Pouf and Circumstance
Philistine Misunderstandings	Preaching to the Converted

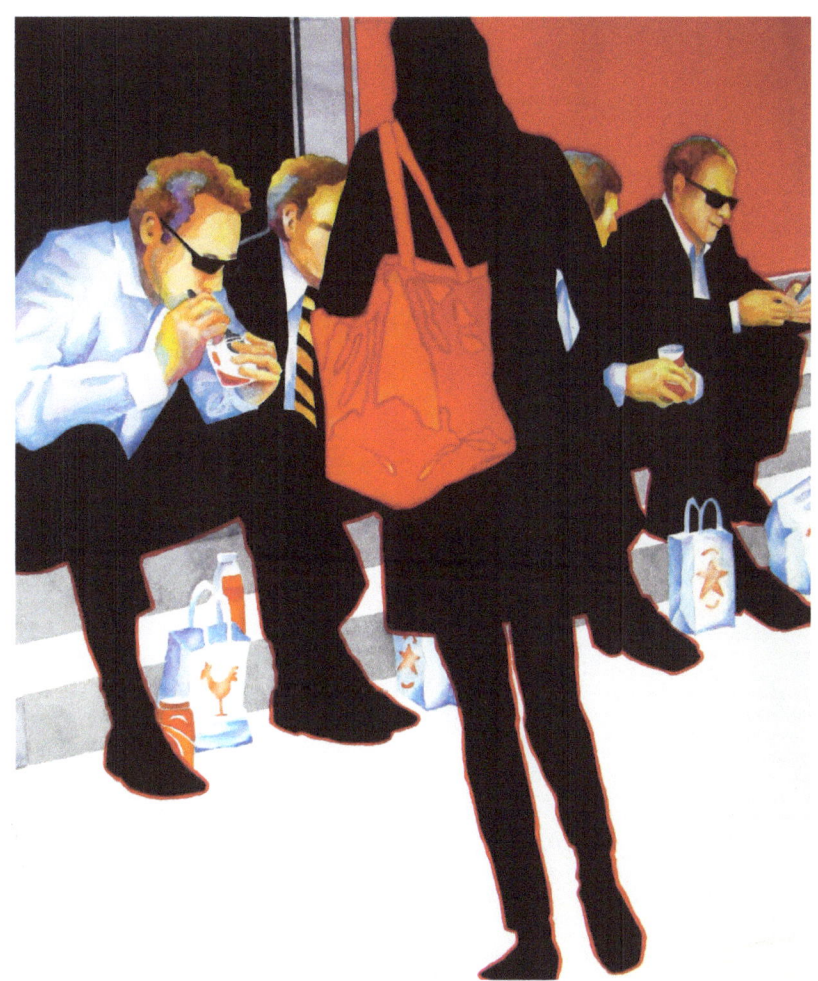

"Manhattan Spring," 29 x 22, watercolor

Preconceived
Predilection for Irony
Premeditated
Preoccupied
Present Tense
Preservation
Press Release
Predisposition
Pretend You Don't See Her
Pretext for a Conversation
Previously Bare Trees
Previously Big News
Previously Blue Circle

Pride and Prejudice
Prism of Events
Private Woods
Profiling
Prologue
Prologue to Fall
Prominently Featured
Propaganda
Protective Coloration
Protections from Real Life
Provisional View
Proxy
Pseudo-realities

Public Offerings
Pull to Inflate Disheveled Elegance
Pumpkin Shell
Punk Rock for Sissies
Purple Haze (other colors?)
Pursuing Perspective
Pursuit of Happiness
Queen of Hearts
Quiet Shadows
Rabbit Ears
Racing Life
Racism, Like all Evil, is Attractive
(Jeff Simon)
Raffish and Louche
Rain Drumming
Raising Expectations
Random Family
Ratty Data
Re... Dressing
Read (Color) Between the Lines
Read Between the Lines
Reading Like a Writer
Real Imitation
Real Life Barging In
Reality and the Imagination
Reality leaves a lot to the imagination.
(John Lennon)
Really Red
Recent History

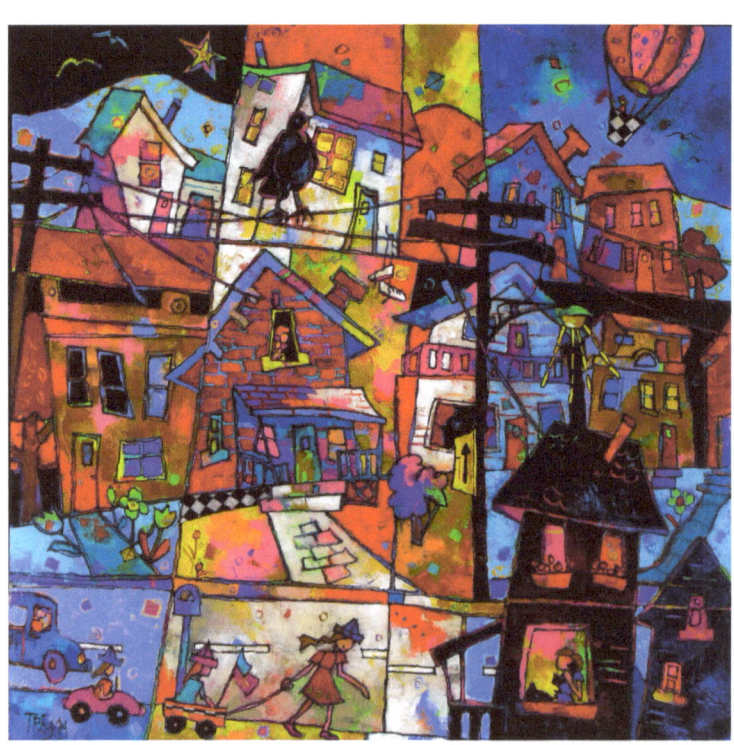

"When Phones Were Heavy and Stayed Home," 24 x 24, acrylics on canvas

Reckless
Reckless Abandon
Recorded Message
Red Coats
Red Necks and Blue Necks
Reduced Abstraction
Reductive Style
Reflection
Reflections
Rehearsal for Life
Rehearsals
Remember the Year I Was Popular?
Remember the Year You Were Popular?
Remembering the Past that Never Was
Remind Me of Who I Am Again
Remote Control
Removing the Adverbs
Reparation
Repetitive Motion
Repetitive Stress Syndrome
Representations
Republican Arithmetic
Republican Opacity
Rescuing Patty Hearst
Resigning from the Herd
Resisting Arrest
Rest in Pieces
Resume
Retail Therapy

Retired Homemaker
  (*Oxymoron*)
Reunion
Rhetorical Colors
Rhetorical Questions
Riding in the Backseat
Right Hand Drawing
Rising Expectations
Risk Being Sorry
Riveting
Road Trip
Road Walkers
Roadhouse Blues
Rocking the Boat
Round Trip
Round Trip talking to Myself
Rowing the Atlantic
Rude Awakening
Rules
Rules of the Game
Rumpus Room
Rumsfeld's Shoes
Rumors
Run Amok
Run and Ask Daddy (if he has any more money)
S&H Green Stamps
Same Trailer, Different Park
Satire
Saturday
Saving Agnes

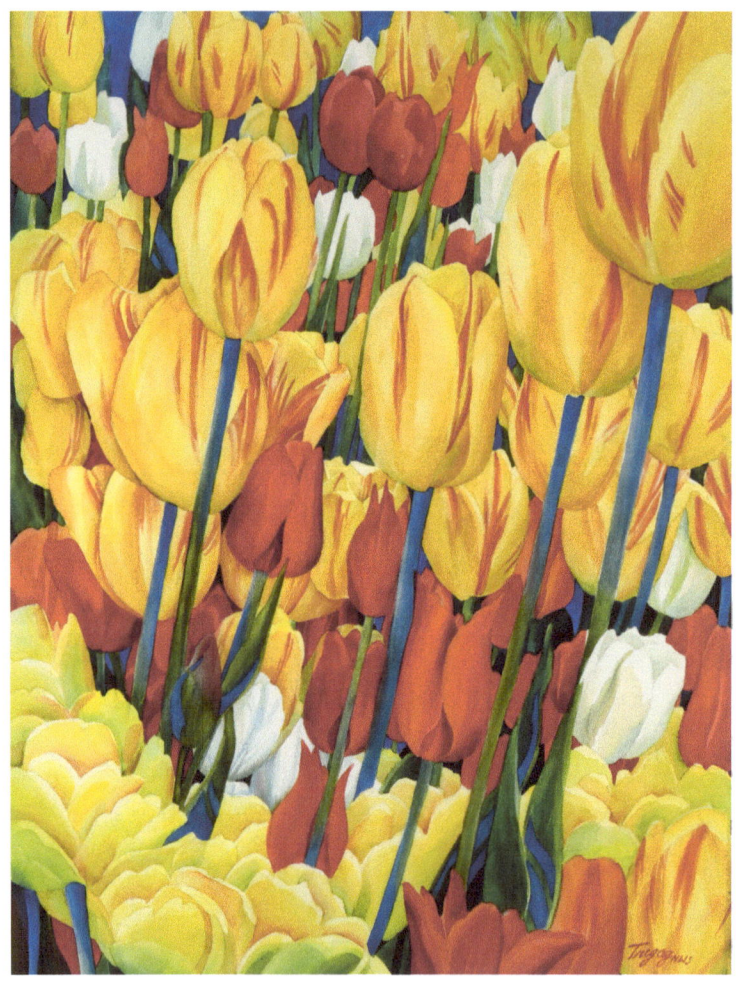
"Someone Else's Garden," 30 x 22, watercolor

Saving Sunshine
Say When
School of Unrestrained Conjecture
School of Untrained Conjecture
Scrapbook
Season's Changes
Seating Arrangements
Second Glance
Second Means of Egress
Second Nature
Second Look
Second Opinion
Second Person Singular
Second Thoughts
Secondhand Pot
Secret
Secrets and Lies
Secular Humorist
Secular Saint
See and Be Seen
See You Later Alligator
Seeing is a Neglected Enterprise
Seems Like Art
Selective Memory
Self-Absorbed
Self-Portrait with Ears *(Mickey Mouse ears)*
Self-Storage
Senior Moment

Serendipitousness
Serial Mom
Serious Comedy
Sex is Different from Gender
Shade
Shadow Layers of Sleep
Shades of Twilight
She Came to Stay
She Said
Shedding Social Conscience
Shortcuts
Should I tell Her?
Side View
Sight Unseen
Sight-lines
Sights Unseen
Silence Between Us
Silence of Small Talk
Silent Attraction
Silent East
Similac
Simple Truths
Sin, Original or Otherwise
Sketchbook Memories
Slander
Seen But Not Heard
Sleep Walking
Sleeping with Howdy Doody
Sleeping with Milton Avery
Sleeping with Milton Bradley
Sleeping with the Dog
Small Change

Small Changes
Small Sacrifice
Smoking Mostly Other People's Dope
Smooth Operator
Snappy Underwear
Snapshot
Slideshow
Social Anxiety
Social Boundaries Before and After
Social Patterns
Society's Fears
Sold Out
Soliloquy
Somber Notes Disregarded
Some Can Whistle
Some Other Garden
Some Stories Don't Have Two Sides
Some Things Never Change
Someone Else's Garden
Something Happened
Something in the Wind
Something to Say
Somewhat Naive
Songs in the Key of Yiddish
Sorry You Asked
Soul
Sound Bites
Sounds
South

Southern Discomfort
Southern Exposure
Southern Gothic
Special People
Spectacular Vernacular
Spar Parts
Spin Cycle
Spring Awakening
Spring Costumes
Spring Incognito
Spring Runoff
Spring Runoff and a New Season
Stained Glass
Standing in Line
Standing Ovation
Staring
Starting from Scratch
Stating the Obvious
Stay Tuned
Still Time
Stir-fry
Story House
Storytelling
Straight Forward, Uncomplicated
Straight Up
Stranger than Fiction
Stay Tuned
Stream of Conscious
Street Gems

Stressed Spelled Backwards (*desserts*)
String Theory (*fiddles*)
Strings Attached
Stuck in the 60's
Subterfuge
Suburban Flotsam
Suburban Nightmare (beaded kitchen)
Suburban Portals (doors, windows)

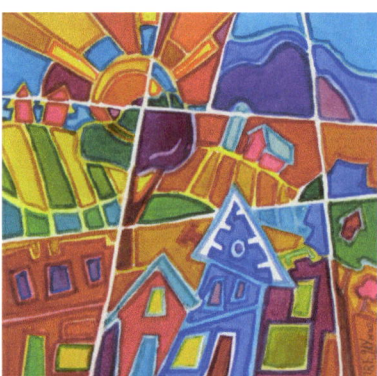
"Eat Your Heart Out Milton Bradly," 6 x 6, watercolor

Suburban Shelter
Sultry Weather
Summer People
Sun Dance
Sunshine Climate Change
Super 8
Surf and Turf
Surfacing

Sushi for Beginners
Suspended Animation
Suspending Disbelief
Suspension of Disbelief
Swimming Pool Season
Syncopated Humor
Table for Two
Table of Concepts
Taking Care of Business
Taking Notes
Talkin' to Myself
Talking Points
Talking to Another Self
Talking to the Dog
Talking to the TV
Tall, White Men
Tangled Circumstance
Tangled Webs
Taste of the Past
Telecommuters
Testimony
Thank Heaven for Dale Evans
Thataway
That Part Was True
That Summer in Paris
That Takes Ovaries
That Way
The A-List
The Age of Insight
The Age of Truthiness
The Amateur Hour
The Amateur Marriage

The Ambiguity of Memory
The American Lover
The American Myth
The American Obsession (the lawn, food)
The Anesthetized Fifties
The Anxiety of Change
The Art Critic
The Beacon
The Beginner's Goodbye
The Big Picture
The Bikini Turns 70
The Blame Game
The Brink
The Call
The Center of Attention
The Chair as a Self-Portrait
The Chick Magnet (a dog)
The Church of Call Waiting
The Color of your Socks
The Comic Tragedy of Human Existence
The Cruelest Month (April)
The Cultural Immune System
The Cultural Trainee
The Culture is Us
The Curfew
The Dare
The Dawn of Aquarius Arrived at 3 PM
The Day Before
The Day Before Everything Happened

The Dew Drop Inn
The Dinner
The Dirty Drug
The Distinguished Guest
The Energy Between Us
The Eastern Shore
The Extrovert
The Fallen and the Saved
The Family Dog
The Fatigue Artist
The Feminist's Daughter
The Fifty Minute Hour
The First Decade
The Fortune Teller
The Fragile World
The Future isn't What It Used to Be
The Girl in the Photo
The Gist of It
The Glimpse
The Grammar of Seeing
The Guest
The Hemingway Solution
The High Cost of Living
The Hippie
The Hipster
The Hokey Pokey Was All That It Was About
The Home Show
The House Next Door
The Icon of the Moment
The Image of Me

The Imperfectionist
The Importance of Being Little
The Insufferable
The Invention of Drawing
The Kitchen
The Last Child in the Woods
The Last Conservative
The Last Democrat Standing
The Last Five Minutes Before Feminism
The Last Generation (to be raised without computers)
The Last Green Sofa
The Last Liberal
The Last of the Green Sofa
The Last Picture Show
The Last Time We Met
The Lay of the Land
The Lives of Others
The Looking Glass
The Low Hanging Fruit
The Lyric
The Lyric Year
The Macho Paradox
The Message
The Microwave Life
The Moment Before
The Movie and the Book
The Movies of My Life
The Names We Give Ourselves
The New Girls
The Next Door Over

The Next Word
The Nick of Time
The Obvious
The Optimist
The Optimist and the Pessimist
The Optimist's Daughter
The Outsider
The Painted Word
  (Tom Wolfe)
The Past in Another Country
The Path Itself
The Point of it All
The Pope Died and Johnny Cash is Dead Too
The Pun Also Rises
The Realist
The Rec Room
The Reluctant Dancer
The Remains of Today
The Replacements
The Return
The Revenge of Thomas Ekins
  (or other artist)
The Revolution Will Not be Televised
The Right Girl for the Job
The Right Outfit
The Risk Pool
The Rumor
The Road Home
The Sea Breathes In and Out
The Search Continues
The Second Child

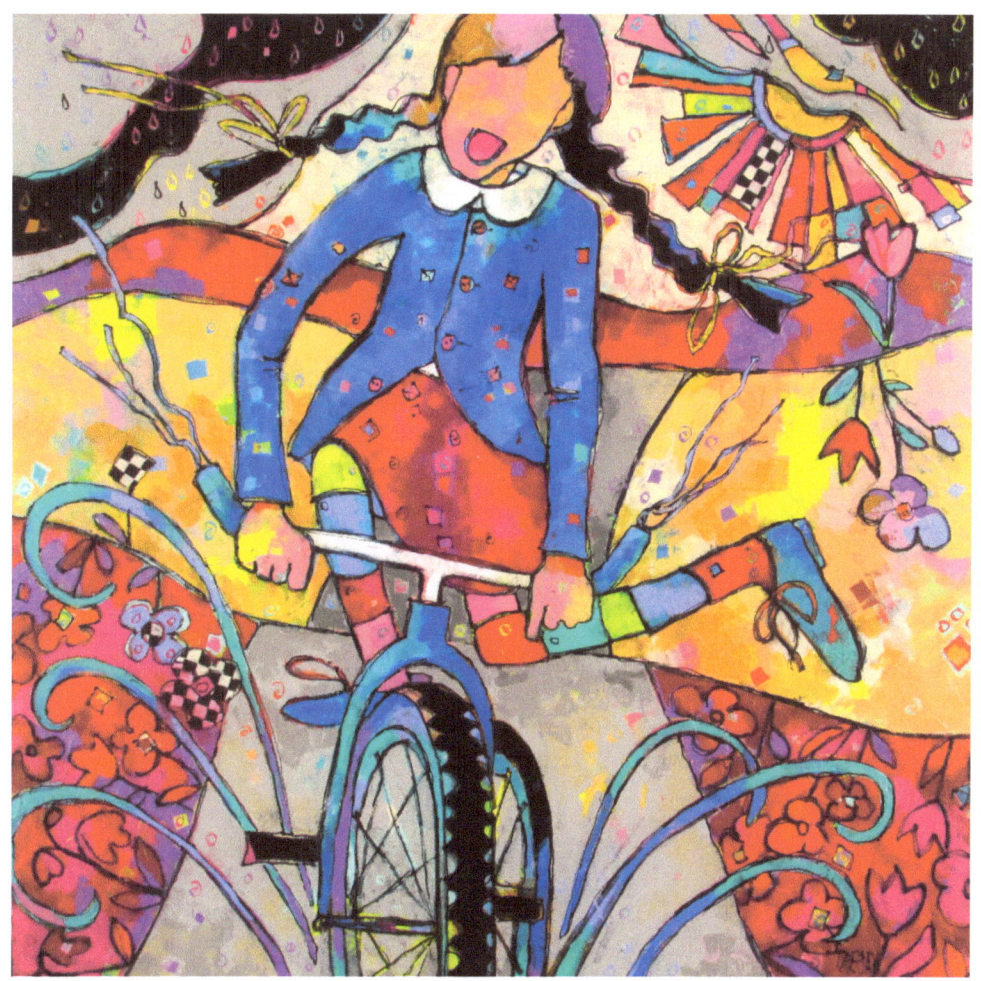
"My Fearless Future," 24 x 24, acrylics on canvas

The Shop Next Door
The Silence of Small Talk
The Situation
The Sixties
The Slacker Generation
The Smile
The Space Between Us
The Starting Point
The Stranger Beside Me
The Storyteller
The Sunday People
The Surface of Things
The Talkies
The Taste of School Paste

The Third Act
The Third Millennium
The Time of Taffeta
The Truth is Stranger than Fiction
The Under Painting
The Visit
The Wait
The Wave
The Whole Story
The Wind at My Back
The World by Half
The Year
The Year that Followed

Then and Now
Then as Now
Then What Happened?
Theoretical Chaos
Therapists, New-agers and Born Again Christians Seldom Blink
There Aren't Any Streakers Anymore
There is a Fine Line Between Righteousness and Self-Righteousness
There is No Main Character in Life
There is No Planet B
These Are The things I Know to be True
These Days Are Ours
Things We Carry *(purse)*
Things We Didn't Know
Things We Do
This and That
This April Tale
This is Not a Portrait
This is Not News
This Way
This Year I Will be Different
Three-Day Weekend
Thrills
Time Flies Over Us and Leaves It's Shadow Behind
Times Alone
To be happy in life, lower your expectations.

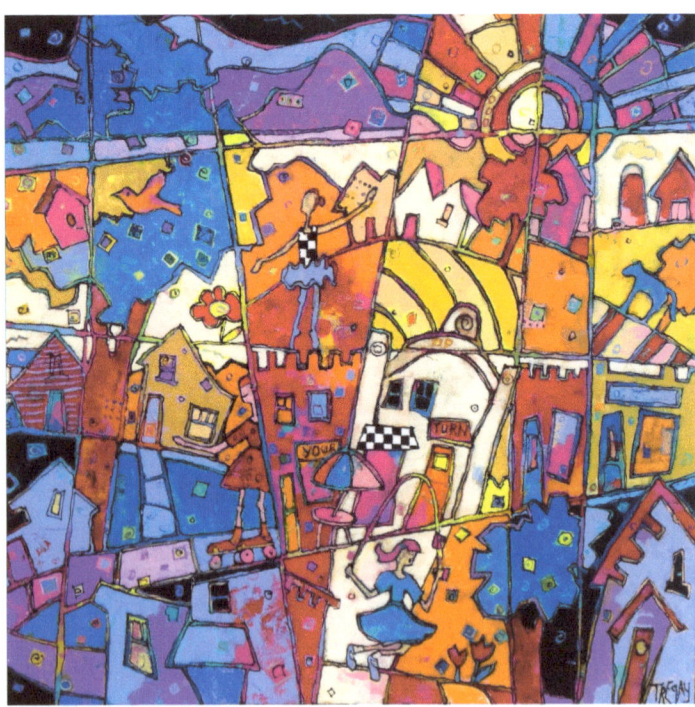

"Everyone Else Lived on a Hill," 24 x 24, acrylics on canvas

Token Male
Tomorrow
Too Far Afield
Too Much of a Good thing
Tossed Salad
Total Ellipse
Touch
Touchy Subject
Touchy Subjects
Train of Thought
Train Spotting
Transitional Moment
Trash
Travel is fatal to racism.
   (Mark Twain)
Travelogue
Tree of Life
Tree Perspective
Trembling in the Wind
Trespassing in Time
Tropism *(flowers turning toward the light)*
True Fiction
True North
True to Form
True to Life
Truth, Fiction and White Lies
Turn Signals
Tunnel Vision
Turning Pages
Turning Reality into Appearances
Turning the Tables

Turning up the Rhetoric
Two Blocks, then Left
Two Hours
Unannounced
Unbroken Circle
Undeniable Special Report
Undercurrents
Under the Bed Monsters Wink
Under the Influence
Undergarments
Undisclosed Location
Uneasy Relation
Unexpected
Unfinished
Unfinished Sentence
Un-gated Community
Un-hatched Chickens
Un-hatched Chicks
Unhinged
Unintended Consequences
Uninteresting Absurdities of Being Alive
   (Larry Rivers)
Unknown Americans
Unprotected Art
Unprotected Music
Unreal Estate
Unresolved Episodes
Unspoken
Unsung Notes (on a staff strung between us)
Unstoppable

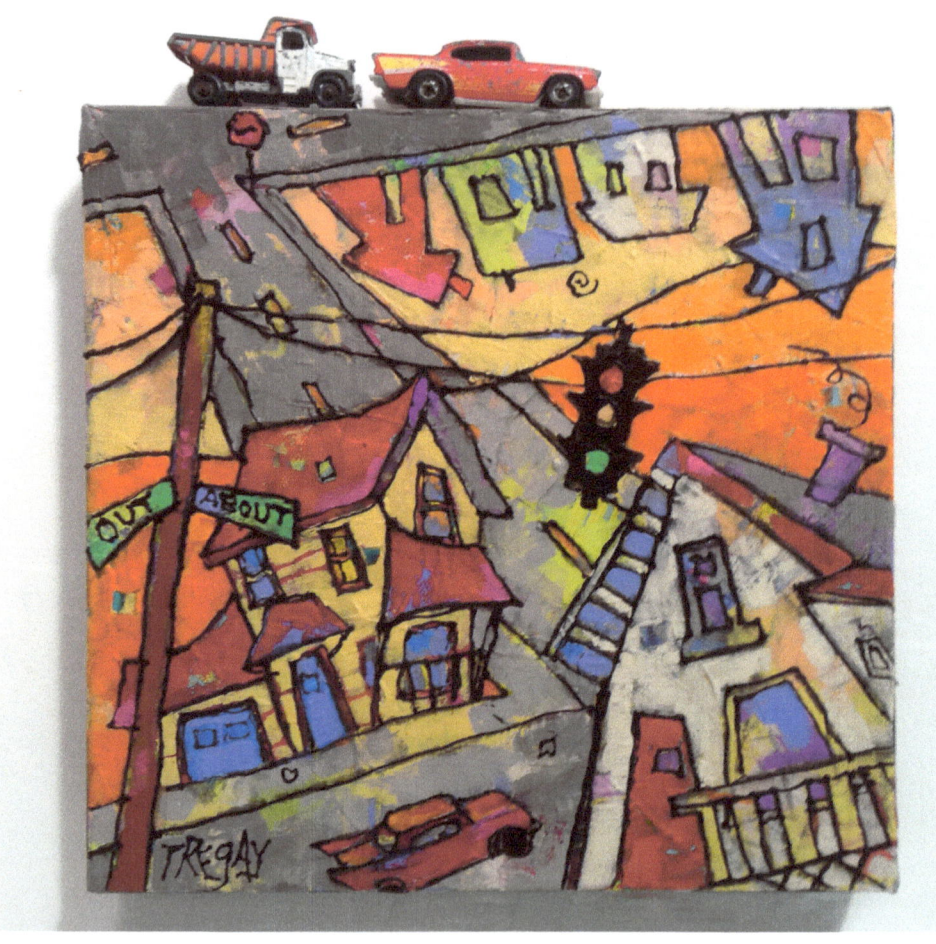

"Out and About," 10 X 10 acrylics on canvas, with Matchbox Cars

Until the Real Thing Comes Along
Until Then
Urban Fiction
Urban Shelter
Urban Tattoo *(sounds)*
UR Here
Valentine
Vanguard Artist
Vanguards of Summer
Variations on a Theme
Vermilion Street
Veronica in the Cloth
View from the Backseat
Violence of the Real
Virtual Pink
Visual Language
Visual Languages
Visual Theater
Voice Recognition
Voices in My Head
Void
Vortex
Vying for Dominance
Waiting
Wake Up Little Susie
Walkin' the Dog
Walking and Talking
Walking the Fine Line
Walking Tour
Wash, Rinse, Repeat
Wasted Time

Watch Your Step
Watchful Waiting
Watching and Waiting
Water Table
Watercolorful.com
We all Chase the Foreseeable Future
We have met the enemy, and he is us. *(Pogo/Walt Kelly)*
We Were in Love with the Kennedys, but They Died
We'll Always Have Paris
Weather
Weaving and Braiding
Wednesday *(or any day)*
Weeks and Weeks
Well Look Who's Here
Well, I feel like 103
West
What a Field Day for the Heat
What are Little Girls Made of?
What Are You Looking At?
What Did I Say?
What Did She Say?
What Frida Wore
What I Had Before I Had You
What I know for Sure
What if Introverts Ruled the World
What if the Hokey Pokey is All That It's About?
What Remains

What She Saw
What to Leave Out
What was I Thinking?
What Was That About?
What We Keep
What we Lost
What Would a Hippie Do?
What Would A Hipster Do?
What's ya Lookin' at?
When Donna Reid was a Verb
When God was a Woman
When I Grow Up I Want to be Just Like Jasper Johns
When I Lived in Modern Times
When I was Last in Love
When it Was Over
When Jukeboxes Took Quarters
When Telephones Were Heavy and Stayed Home
When the Drummers were Women
When the Hokey Pokey was All That it was About
When We Liked Ike
When We went to the Farm in 2nd Grade, We Walked
Where is the Audience?
Where or When
Where to Begin
Which or Both
While England Sleeps
While I was Gone

Whipper-Snapper Nerd
Whispered Betrayals
White Lies and Other Stories
White Teeth
Who Needs Drugs When You Have Sex and Rock & Roll?
Who's Afraid of Color?
Who's Afraid of Coloring?
Who's Afraid of Garlic?
Who's Afraid of Polka Dots?
Who's Afraid of Purple?
Who's Afraid of Red and Blue?
Who's Afraid of Red, Yellow and Blue?
Who's Opinion Counts?
Why Chase the Foreseeable Future?
Why I go to the Movies Alone
Why She Went Home
Wildfire
Will Allegory Kill Art?
Windblown
Windfall
Window of Silence
Window or Aisle?
Windows on the Mind
Windswept
Winter Keeps on Happening
Winter Solstice
Wish You Were Here
Wit and Mischief
Within the Lines

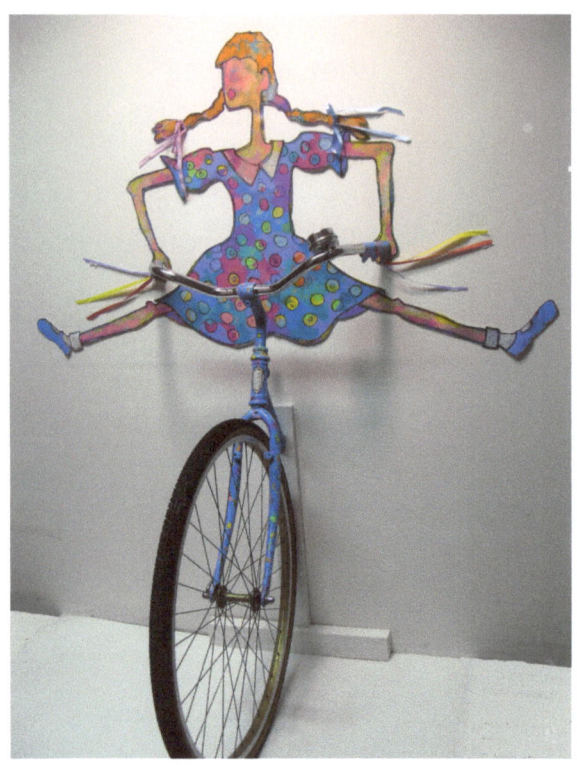

"Frequent Flyer," acrylic on canvas with bicycle part

Without Consent
Women and Children First
Women Last
Without Irony or Agenda
Women in Paris
Word of Mouth
Work or Art
Working the Impala
World View
World's Window

Yesterday
Yellow, Yellow Catch a Fellow
You Can Do Anything, Just Have Good Shoes On
You Can't Argue with Your Scrapbook
(Andy Warhol)
You're in the Wong Movie
YRU Here?
You Thought It Was funny, But It Was Really Ironic

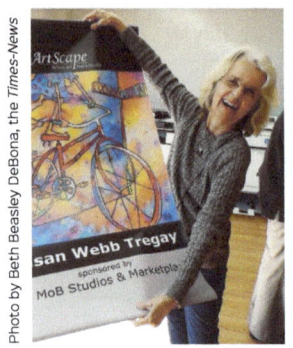

Susan Webb Tregay, an award-winning, signature member of the American Watercolor Society and the National Watercolor Society, is the author of *Master Disaster, Five Ways to Rescue Desperate Watercolors* [North Light, 2007]. Her acrylic series, "Art for Adult Children," has been honored with three solo museum shows. She teaches workshops and juries exhibitions around the country and spent four years as the art critic for a Rockford, IL, newspaper. More of her art can be seen at tregay.com and SusanWebbTregay.com.

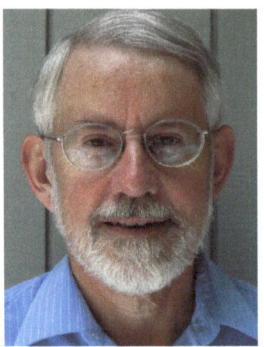

George W. Tregay is an avid reader and spotter of potential painting titles. A career aerospace engineer, he currently does energy audits for school systems, fire halls and non-profits.

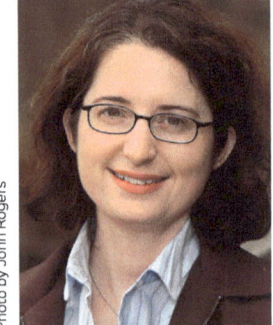

Sarah Tregay is a graphic designer and author of *Love and Leftovers* and *Fan Art* [HarperCollins 2012 and 2014]. For more about her books, visit sarahtregay.com.